NETWORKING
for RESULTS

Foreword by
Dr. George C. Fraser

NETWORKING
for RESULTS

Unlocking Your Success through Strategic Connections

LINUS OKORIE MFR

Publishing services by:

EVANGELISTA MEDIA & CONSULTING
Via Maiella, 1 66020 San Giovanni Teatino (CH) – Italy
publisher@evangelistamedia.com
www.evangelistamedia.com

For Worldwide Distribution, Printed in Europe

1 2 3 4 5 6 / 26 25 24 23

DEDICATION

I dedicate this book to my wife, Nkiru Linus Okorie, and my three children: Ebubechukwu Linus-Okorie, Chukwuebuka Linus-Okorie, and Chimamaka Linus-Okorie.

I also extend this dedication to my mother, Susanna Okorie.

Furthermore, this book is for anyone who reads it, in the hope that they may be equipped in their journey of networking their way to the top.

ACKNOWLEDGMENTS

I am grateful to the many individuals who have made the journey of writing *Networking for Results* not just possible but deeply rewarding. Each of you has been a divine gift, enriching both my life and the work itself.

First and foremost, my deepest gratitude goes to God, the guiding force behind my life and work. The aspiration to grow in understanding His plan for me drives me forward.

To my wife, Nkiru, your enduring support has been my rock, providing me with peace and stability as I strive to develop leaders. My children, Ebubechukwu, Chukwuebuka, and Chimamaka, you illuminate my life and fuel my purpose.

I cherish the memory of my late father, who believed in the power of education and set me on my path. My mother, and sister Olive, your ceaseless support and belief have been invaluable.

Special recognition goes to Chief Chris Asoluka, Mazi Sam Ohu-abunwa MON, Mr. Arah Nebolisa, Dr. Ndi Onuekwusi, Dr. Godknows Igali MON, Engr. Charles Okoro, Late Mr. Gamaliel Onosode OFR, Prof. Pat Utomi, Late Mr. Chudi Onuzo, and Mr. Polycarp Ajoko. Your continued support, both financial and moral, has been invaluable.

A special mention is due for my spiritual mentors. Thank you, Bishop David Oyedepo, Bishop Dickson Olorunda, Late Pastor Taiwo and Bimbo Odukoya, and Apostle Joshua Selman for your spiritual guidance and prayers. To Chidinma Olarewaju for encouraging me to share my networking principles to the world.

To my friends, your steadfast love and support has enriched my life in ways words cannot express.

I'm also grateful to the board and executives of GOTNI. Your collective commitment to our mission and tireless efforts keep the dream alive.

A heartfelt thank-you to everyone who lent their skills to this book. Blessing Okebe, Val Okafor, Hephzibah Emereole, Jerry Kanyinebi, Samuel Isiwu. Your meticulous reviews and contributions have been invaluable.

Further thanks go to the team at Evangelista Media & Consulting; your decade-long publishing expertise has been instrumental in polishing this book to its current form, and your steadfast work has transformed it into a tool to impact nations for everlasting change.

Each one of you has made a unique and indelible impact on this project, and for that, I am eternally grateful.

FOREWORD BY
DR. GEORGE C. FRASER

The Power of the Human Connection

For over 40 years, I have spent time researching and teaching networking. I have seen many people who have become very successful in life as a result of the support and networks of the high-quality people they have met at conferences, workshops, marriage ceremonies, birthdays, church, dinners, and travel.

It takes a lot of people for you to have a successful career: people who provide you with ideas, information, connect you to others, and sponsor you or your ideas. To build this type of network, your networking activity needs to be strategic. To create the type of network that empowers your ambition, you must make deliberate and intentional efforts. Understanding the power of the human connection has become a moral, spiritual, and strategic skill of leaders to own in the 21st century. Leaders don't build businesses or organizations, they connect with the right people, then build and bond with them, and those people build their business and organization. That is how God has designed the system for communal success – everyone wins. All the support you may need is in the hands of someone within your country, city, or beyond the shores of your country.

A lot of research shows that professional networks will always lead to more opportunities, business, and great knowledge of advancing the vision and goals of the brands they represent through great ideas that are gotten through great interactions with different levels and kinds of people from across the world. Most of us are ambivalent about networking. We know that it's important to our professional success, yet we find it very challenging to network. But it is not. It is part of God's design and plan for all of us. Simply listen, learn, and be obedient to the power of the human connection and you cannot fail.

Dr. Linus Okorie MFR, whom I have known for over a decade, has put together powerful and globally tested principles that will inspire you to take the concept of networking very seriously. These strategies would help you overcome your aversion to networking, even if you are an introvert. You will become very effective at building relationships that bear fruit for you and create a win-win for everyone.

It is a must-read for everyone who desires to lead in extraordinary ways.

Dr. George Fraser is the visionary and founder of the Black Business Hall of Fame and Museum and the Global Center for Black Entrepreneurial Leadership. He is a 7-time bestselling author, global speaker, and an award-winning entrepreneur. He is the Founder/President of FraserNet, Inc.(1987). He has received over 350 awards and citations to include a two-time recipient of the Presidential Lifetime Achievement Award (Obama 86 & Biden 22) He's an inductee into the Minority Business Hall of Fame & Museum (2011). Dr. Fraser has received 3 Honorary Doctorates, an Ambassadorship and Chaplaincy.

CONTENTS

INTRODUCTION

Chris Jemba is 22 years old. He is the oldest of three children and is about to graduate from a university. Luckily for him, he has no pressures from home since his parents are able to conveniently cater to their children's needs. Yet, Chris is pressured nonetheless. He is a man now and there are expectations. Subliminal, yet very real and invisibly palpable. Immediately after he finishes his final exam and has completed school, without saying it out loud, everyone expects him to get a job, leave his parents' home and move into his own place, buy a car sooner or later, grow in his career by being a valuable player at the company where he works and thereby climb the ladder, get married at some point, have children and father them—the list goes on. No one says all this to him, but he knows they all expect as much or more from him. He is pressured. Anxious. Where and how does he start?

Chris Jemba is not alone in this quagmire of unspoken expectations. In fact, Chris Jemba is all of us. Every human being. You. Me. We are all Chris Jemba, only we are at different stages of his journey. You may be in college right now, just starting your career, or you may have had a career for a few years now. Maybe you have started your own company and have a family, or perhaps you are in the eve years of your sojourn on earth. Nevertheless, you are somewhere on the parallel of Chris's life.

And we all want the same thing—to make progress. To advance in life and get the best of what is possible with our respective quests. We all want to be happy, and that means making progress at the things we set our hearts to accomplish.

Tony Robbins, successful author and coach, rightly says, "I can tell you the secret of happiness in one word: progress." I agree.

But how do we achieve progress? How can we move our lives from where we are now to where we want to be? Is there a one-size-fits-all solution for getting ahead in life? Is there a "one thing" that if we adopt and apply ourselves to, we are guaranteed of success?

I dare say yes, there is.

That one thing is *people*.

When you get the right people in your life, as many of them as you possibly can, you can be assured that you will almost always accomplish whatever you set out to do—provided you put in the necessary work, of course.

People are assets. People provide opportunities. People provide leverage. People provide resources. People allow for delegation and distribution of tasks for achieving an objective. People allow you to multiply and maximize your time. You need people. Always.

This is why we are discussing *Networking for Results*. I congratulate you for picking up this book to read, because you are about to be armed with one of the most potent strategies for getting anything you want out of life. And this discourse is especially important now because we are living in dire times. Resources are shrinking. Opportunities are diminishing. And the scarce resources and opportunities that are available are in such a high demand that it takes a well thought out plan to gather all you need to succeed. Everyone is scrambling for a piece of the lean pie. What are the odds that you will be one with pie on your plate?

There is a better way than scrambling and hustling to get what you need, which is what I share with you in this book. That better way is simply how *to befriend the holders of the scarce resources and opportunities* so they call you themselves and share with you without any of the hassling. Wouldn't your life be much easier that way? Wouldn't it be a better way to get the job, contract, new business, etc. that you want? Wouldn't that be a better way to smash your goals every time?

This book is about is how to leverage relationship currency for progress. You will always need somebody to speak up for you, to hold a door for you and usher you into your next level, to refer you, to expend their influence for you, to support your growth, to fund your business or project, etc. This book is about how to find those people, connect with them, and stay top-of-mind so they remember and help you when you need it the most.

Are you ready?

Turn the next page now and let's begin.

CHAPTER 1

LIFE'S GRAND DESIGN

We Are Creatures of Interdependency

No one can accomplish anything by themselves. The world was designed for interconnectivity and interdependency. As the famous poem cites, "No man is an island, entire of itself; every man is a piece of the continent, a part of the main."[9] Every whole is a function of its constituent parts. Every successful man and woman are what they are because of the support received on their way to that height. Everyone has been helped by someone else somewhere and sometime. Nobody, no matter how high up they are today, attained their goals solely by their own effort. No such person exists or has ever existed. Not in this material world.

The principle governing the physical world disallows that possibility, and you either align with it or resign yourself to achieving nothing in life. In fact, even if you choose the latter, you still cannot escape being helped. It's just how life was designed. It is the grand design.

To start, your mother carried you in her womb for nine whole months, feeding, protecting, and nurturing you. That was help. Then she endured the unfathomable pain of giving birth to you. Another help. Again, she and your father fed you, clothed you, sheltered you, protected you, provided for your needs, taught you how to do life, educated you, etc., all the way until you became an adult and able to care for yourself.

And along the way you were helped by teachers, relatives, friends, neighbors, strangers, and others—to varying degrees. Then someone referred you to the notice of a job offer, you applied and got it. Another person introduced you to the cute lady or handsome gentlemen who stole your heart and you later married. Still, someone told you about a business opportunity that turned out to be very profitable, bolstering your financial status…the list is endless. How then can anyone conveniently say they are self-made, or that they don't need people in their lives, or disregard investing in growing their network? Friend, life was designed for interdependence.

Notice that in the two illustrations that started this chapter, both speak to the infallibility and efficacy of this grand design of life. The food chain is a testament to the interconnectivity of nature, and the seed analogy speaks to the prudence of investing in growing your network.

Anybody armed with this principle has potential to thrive at unprecedented levels. Their potential is limitless. They can dare to do big things and be confident that they will achieve them, because they understand how to leverage the assets that people are toward accomplishing their objectives. Trust me, the ability to network is real power. I have tasted and proven it, and I have no intention of ever letting go of it during my lifetime.

Everything you want to accomplish has likely been accomplished by someone somewhere. Every system you want to create is probably existing already. So why spend yourself trying to reinvent an existing wheel when you can simply leverage relationships and get what you want? This is why it is important for people to know that networking is an essential skill not just for survival but for making progress.

The Relationship Currency

Every vision, no matter how lofty and inviting, needs people to accomplish it. Visioners are never capable enough to accomplish the vision alone; they always need the contributions of other people. Usually, not just anyone, but people with the requisite skills and committed hearts, willing to drive the growth they collectively seek.

Unfortunately, we are not always as successful as hoped, especially in the early stages of conceiving and driving a vision. Not many people have the capacity to catch a vision in its seed stage and commit themselves to its accomplishment. But more than that, every leader or visioner must acknowledge their need of the cooperation and participation of others in achieving their dreams and goals.

No matter what you want to achieve in life—in business, career, politics, social development, and the like, you need people. People are assets. The opportunity you are seeking will happen only when you find and connect with the right person or persons with the capacity and network to open the door for you. Until you do, your aspirations will thrive only inside your head.

So, your primary job after conceiving a vision is to find and connect with the right people you need. They vary depending on what you are seeking to achieve, but settle it in your heart for now that you need people. This is why we network. It is why I wrote this book: to show you how to network for results, particularly in the 21st century world.

Finding the right people to aid your vision is the frustration of vision. But it is a solvable frustration.

A Day in the Jungle

Every morning, the sun rises from the east. It's a given. That is the design of nature. The sun rises in the east and sets in the west. Every day and night. But the interesting thing is that the sun doesn't rise and set for mere aesthetic reasons or to announce its magnificence; it shows up to perform an important function—the kind life on earth depends on to continue.

Scientists estimate that sunlight takes about eight and a half minutes to reach the earth. They also attribute the convenient conditions of living on earth to the earth's relatively perfect positioning to the sun, in regard to distance. Hence, life on earth relies heavily on the sun, especially its light and heat.

Light from the sun performs very many functions for our planet. It is so important that if the sun decides to go on a vacation, nine minutes later the Earth will be in darkness—that is if it is daytime where you are. If you are in night time, a deep darkness will be instant. Also, photosynthesis will stop immediately. This means that plants will no longer be able to produce their own food and will soon start to die. The animals and humans who rely on plants to get their own food will eventually die as well. More so, global temperatures will start to fall until such a time when most organisms cannot survive the cold; species will die out as they each reach their temperature thresholds.

That said, when the sun rises in the morning, it is nature's smile on the jungle. First, plants receive the sunlight and use it to manufacture their own food, in a process called photosynthesis. Soon, the grasshopper pays the grass a necessary visit to explore its freshness. The grass now has energy because it has been "fed," having produced its own food, whereas the grasshopper needs energy to survive and go about its day. To get energy, it feeds off the grass. And when it is energized, it hops off and about in the jungle.

But today may just be the grasshopper's unlucky day. Later, still pumped with energy from the food it consumed, it misses a hop and falls into the waiting mouth of a frog. The frog was hungry, now lunch is served. It's a good day like every other. Well, is it? Or maybe just for now.

Now energized, the frog leaps and croaks around. It is in its habitat after all. It has been fed for the day and received its share of the energy, made possible in the jungle by the sun. It is in its community, among its kind. But none of them realize an intruder nearby. It is the snake. He, too, wants a share of the energy going around. Unfortunately, the frog is sentenced by nature to provide for him. The grasshopper served him; now the frog must forward the gesture to the snake. So it becomes early dinner for the snake.

The snake, like the frog, swallows its food, and then waits quietly for the food to decompose inside and provide the energy its body needs to function. The snake foolishly lays in an open area, becoming easy prey for a hawk.

For each in the scenario, from the grass to the hawk, it was a good day—all thanks to the sun. The sun supplied light. The grass utilized it to produce its own food (this is why plants are called producers in the ecosystem). Then the consumers (creatures) took turns to take in and give out the energy. But only the hawk ended the day alive, and the cycle continues every day until the day when the hawk finally dies. Then it becomes food for other kinds of organisms, called decomposers. Decomposers are microscopic organisms, in this case mostly bacteria, that feed off dead animals and decompose their bodies for the earth to absorb as nutrients that will eventually serve plants' growth. Now the cycle is complete, starting with the plant and returning to the plant again—the sun being the enabler.

In basic science, this is called the food chain, which shows the transfer of energy from one organism to another through food. This results in a balanced ecology, transferring energy and nutrients, as well as population control within the ecosystem. Of course, if you recall your basic biology, the organisms listed here are only examples. Every organism, including humans, participate in the food chain one way or another.

A Tree Forms a Forest

You may have heard the old saying that a tree does not make a forest. Do you believe that? I don't.

Yes, one tree alone does not constitute a forest; I agree. But that is true only if you think short-term. A major characteristic of great leaders is that they are long-term in their thinking and perspective. This is why they have an uncanny ability to identify potential in its raw form, forecast what it could be in the near or distant future, and harness their power and resources to make the forecast a reality. This is exactly what nature does with a seed.

Take an orange seed for example. An orange fruit is estimated to have an average of ten seeds. So, say I gift you an orange fruit; in truth, I just gave you a fortune with transgenerational implications—little as that is in your hand. But of course what we all do is peel off the rind and enjoy the juice and the flesh of the fruit, then mindlessly throw away the seeds and everything else.

Contrarily, let's presume that you throw those orange seeds in your backyard and by some happenstance one germinates. And somehow it escapes the tyranny of humans—either you or someone in your home, such that it is not trampled upon or rooted out. Three years down the line, it yields its first fruits.

According to Wikifarmer,[1] "the average healthy and mature orange tree produces 200-350 oranges. However, experienced orange farmers after years of practice can harvest between 400 to 600 oranges per tree." So, all you need do after your first harvest—from your "accidental" orange tree that grew in your backyard—is to replant the seeds of the harvested oranges on a large expanse of land and allow another three years to pass.

Let's do some math. Say your first yield was the base estimate of 200 oranges. Multiplying that by the average seed estimate of 10 would give you 2,000 seeds. That is a whopping potential of 2,000 orange trees resulting from only one seed some three years ago.

Also according to Wikifarmer: "Under a dense planting system, in which there are 400 trees per hectare, the expected yield of an experienced farmer would be 40-50 tons per hectare." With this, you have either of two options: become a supplier of orange fruits to fruit drinks manufacturers or become a fruit drinks manufacturer yourself. Whichever you do, when I gave you an orange fruit as a gift, I truly gave you a lifetime fortune—if only you recognized its inherent potential.

So, does a tree make a forest? We both know the true answer now.

Case Studies of Prominent Figures in Nigeria Who Utilized Networking to Succeed

Chief Dele Momodu

Chief Dele Momodu is a well-known Nigerian journalist, publisher, and businessman. He used networking as a key tool to build his career and influence. Momodu established connections with influential figures in the media and entertainment industry, which helped him launch his publication, "Ovation International." By leveraging these connections, he gained access to exclusive interviews and events, contributing to the magazine's success. Furthermore, he used his network to venture into politics and humanitarian work, showcasing the power of connections in various spheres[2].

Dr. Ngozi Okonjo-Iweala, GCON

Dr. Ngozi Okonjo-Iweala, a renowned economist and diplomat, achieved remarkable success through strategic networking. Her extensive network within international organisations, such as the World Bank and various governments, played a pivotal role in her appointment as the Director-General of the World Trade Organization (WTO). Dr. Okonjo-Iweala's ability to connect with global leaders and garner their support was instrumental in her becoming the first African and first woman to hold this prestigious position[3].

Mr. Tony Elumelu, CFR

Mr. Tony Elumelu is a prominent Nigerian entrepreneur and philanthropist who used networking to build his business empire. He established strong connections within the financial sector, notably with United Bank for Africa (UBA), where he served as CEO. Through strategic partnerships and relationships with stakeholders in the African business community, Mr. Elumelu expanded his influence and became a key advocate for entrepreneurship and economic development in Africa, particularly through his Tony Elumelu Foundation[4].

Prof. Pat Utomi

Prof. Pat Utomi, an economist, professor, and entrepreneur, utilised networking to excel in academia, business, and politics. He formed valuable connections with fellow scholars and experts in his field, contributing to his distinguished academic career. Additionally, his networking skills were crucial in his involvement in various policy and political initiatives. Prof. Utomi's ability to collaborate and build alliances with like-minded individuals and organisations has been a driving force behind his multifaceted success[5].

Mr. Nduka Obaigbena, CON

Mr. Nduka Obaigbena is a media mogul and entrepreneur who harnessed the power of networking to establish the ThisDay newspaper and the Arise News television network. His ability to connect with influential figures both nationally and internationally facilitated partnerships and investments in the media industry. Mr. Obaigbena's network played a significant role in positioning his media outlets as prominent players in the Nigerian and global media landscape[6].

General Ibrahim Badamasi Babangida, GCFR

General Ibrahim Babangida, a former Nigerian military leader, used networking to navigate the complex world of Nigerian politics and military affairs. His ability to cultivate relationships with key military and political figures helped him rise to power and maintain a significant influence during his time as Nigeria's president. General Babangida's networking skills allowed him to establish and solidify his position in the country's political landscape[7].

Late High Chief Raymond Dokpesi

Late High Chief Raymond Dokpesi was a prominent Nigerian media magnate known for his influential role in the media industry. Networking played a pivotal role in his journey to success. Initially sponsored by Alhaji Bamanga Tukur during his undergraduate studies, Chief Dokpesi's early connections paved the way for his future endeavours. His most notable networking achievement was the establishment of the African Independent Television (AIT) network. Through strategic networking, he secured licences and support for AIT, making it one of Nigeria's leading television networks. His extensive network in politics and business enabled him to shape public opinion and influence national discourse through AIT. The late High Chief Dokpesi's network of contacts also extended to the political arena, where he played a role in shaping political narratives and participating in various political activities. His influence in both media and politics demonstrated how networking could be a powerful tool for success and impact in Nigeria. Despite his passing away, his legacy in the media industry and his success story underscore the importance of building and leveraging networks to achieve prominence and excel in one's chosen field. His contributions continue to serve as an inspiration to aspiring media entrepreneurs and business leaders in Nigeria[8].

The list of prominent figures in Nigeria who have mastered the art of networking and utilised it to become successful can go on and on. However, the important thing to note is that these individuals serve as prime examples of how networking can be a crucial factor in achieving success and making a lasting impact in various fields, be it journalism, international diplomacy, entrepreneurship, academia, media, or politics. Their ability to forge meaningful connections and leverage them effectively contributed significantly to their accomplishments.

Now, why do we network? Or, more personally, why should you network? The answer to this question is the thrust of the next chapter's focus.

Summary Thoughts

1. Life was designed for interdependence.

2. No human being, no matter how highly placed or accomplished they are, is ever truly self-made. We are all products of other people's contributions.

3. Finding the right people to aid your vision is the frustration of vision. But it is a solvable frustration.

4. No matter what you want to achieve in life—in business, career, politics, social development, etc.—you need people. People are assets. The opportunity you are seeking will happen only when you find and connect with the right person or persons with the capacity and network to open the door for you.

5. With time, effort, and consistency, a tree can become a forest.

ACTIONABLE TAKEAWAYS JOURNAL

CHAPTER 2

THE HEART
OF NETWORKING

Having established our intrinsic need of other people's contribution to our growth and progress, let us now explore how to secure their help. The term for this is "networking." It is a business term that applies to building valuable relationships that can potentially aid someone's growth, progress, and development. It applies whether you are building a business or seeking to advance your career. Networking is a necessity.

Networking is the art of creating connections and broadening your scope of influence, to the end of mutually rewarding gains. It is making yourself more influential by having valuable people in your space. More than that, it is positioning yourself to give out quality value.

Put another way, networking is the act of making business contacts for purposes beyond the initial reason for the contact. This means networking is not solely for preplanned purposes alone;

you can network with people for purposes of having a thriving relationship with them that could later evolve in unforeseeable ways. Networking is a deliberate effort at meeting people, building relationships, sharing opportunities, and exchanging value.

This is one of the key secrets of high flyers in any field of human endeavor. They understand that networking is a strategy for getting ahead, creating and leveraging opportunities, and making significant strides. Networking is a skill, a requisite ability for thriving and achieving success.

So, if you want to excel, smash your business or career goals, climb to new heights, explore new horizons, find and leverage opportunities, you must become adept at networking. Networking is a master key for opening doors of advancement in different areas of life.

There appears to be a gross misunderstanding of what networking is. This misunderstanding cuts across the circles of seasoned professionals and young professionals alike. I find it very disturbing. It is a way of thinking that skews the idea of networking on the path of selfishness and self-aggrandizement. It is an approach to networking that is parasitic in nature, which is a total deviation from what networking truly is. And this erroneous thinking and approach is the reason many people fail to experience the awesome gains of networking in their lives. Allow me to correct your perspective here, and thereby help you.

If you were keen to observe my definitions of networking in the previous paragraphs, you may have noticed that I deliberately chose my words. I did that on purpose to ensure that you don't miss the true concept of networking and join the bandwagon of a misconstrued notion. I used words including, "sharing," "exchange," "mutual gains," and other specific words and phrases. That is because networking is never a one-sided engagement. Networking never thrives if it is solely for the purpose of serving one person's selfish needs or desires. No, networking is for mutual benefits. Networking is about giving—fundamentally.

In its truest essence, networking is an act undertaken by two or more people with the intent to give and receive value. That is, each person is expected to approach the relationship with a mindframe to give first, not to take. Remember the old Bible injunction that says it is more blessed to give than to receive? It aptly applies here. And the reason is simple. When you are networking as a business owner or an upwardly mobile professional, you are seeking to meet people of similar cadre or above you—of like mind, interests, and inclinations. These are the kinds of people with a potential to share ideas, information, or opportunities that could forge you forward. So be careful to find and connect with them.

The converse is also true, that others are careful to find people of like mind, interests, and inclinations with whom to connect. They are convinced as you are that such people will more than likely aid their growth and progress through assorted value sharing. Sadly, many people are blind to this fact. They think selfishly, only about themselves and their needs, and not about what the other person might need. As a result, when they connect with a new contact, all they think about is what they can get, what they can market or pitch to the person, how they can dig into their pocket or contact list. That is a repugnant way to approach networking. If you have that mindset, trust me, you will undermine the power and possibilities of networking and it will not serve you well. Networking is first and foremost about giving. It is about serving. It is an opportunity to provide value to another.

This is the catch. When you are helpful to someone, you compel that person to be helpful to you. If you give value, the other person will feel impressed to return the gesture. It is like sowing a seed that will yield a harvest, all conditions being checked. Remember that life was designed for independency. You need the next person by you just as much as they need you. We all need each other to maximize our human experience. This is the height of living. It is why we network, to expand our social net so that we can share the value we have to support others and get the value we need in return. Take this factor out of the human experience and living will be a burden. Very boring.

In the remaining portion of this chapter, I will delve deep into and examine in detail the prevalent misunderstanding about networking.

Networking Is Not a Self-Serving Activity

Networking has become a buzzword in the business world. It is often associated with self-promotion and the quest for personal gain. While networking does involve building relationships with people, it is not solely about advancing oneself. Networking is about creating mutually beneficial relationships that are based on trust, respect, and a willingness to give and receive value.

Unfortunately, there is a common misconception that networking is a self-serving activity. Some people believe that networking is only for people who are looking to advance their careers or grow their businesses. They view networking as a way to gain access to influential people or to get ahead at the expense of others. This is a fundamental misunderstanding of what networking is and what it can do for you.

Networking is not just about taking, it is also about giving. It is about creating value for others and building relationships based on trust and mutual respect. The best networkers are those who are generous with their time, knowledge, and resources. They are always looking for ways to help others, whether it is by introducing them to potential clients, sharing valuable information, or providing a listening ear when needed.

Networking is not a one-sided engagement. It is about creating win-win situations where both parties benefit. The most successful networkers are those who understand this and are willing to invest time and effort in building meaningful relationships with others. They are willing to help others achieve their goals and to share their own knowledge and expertise to create value for others.

One of the biggest misconceptions about networking is that it is only for extroverted people who are comfortable in social situations. While it is true that networking often involves attending events and meeting new people, it is not limited to those who are outgoing or gregarious. In fact, some of the most successful networkers are introverts who excel at building one-on-one relationships with others.

Another misconception about networking is that it is all about exchanging business cards and making small talk. While these things are certainly important, they are not the most important aspects of networking. The real value of networking lies in the relationships that are built over time. These relationships are based on trust, respect, and a willingness to help others.

Networking is not a one-time activity. It is an ongoing process that requires time, effort, and commitment. The best networkers are those who are consistent in their efforts and who are always looking for ways to add value to others. They understand that building relationships takes time, and they are willing to invest that time in order to achieve their goals.

The Key to Mutual Benefits and Long-Term Success

Networking is often viewed as a way to meet people who can help you achieve your goals. However, the most successful networkers understand that it is not about what you can get from others, but what you can give. The act of giving first is crucial in networking and can lead to mutual benefits and long-term success.

When you approach networking with the intent to give, you create a positive impression and build trust with others. People are more likely to want to work with someone who has their best interests in mind and is willing to help them succeed. By being helpful, you establish a reputation as a valuable resource and someone who is worth knowing.

Giving can take many forms in networking. It could be as simple as introducing two people who could benefit from knowing each other or sharing information that could help someone solve a problem. It could also involve volunteering your time and expertise to help a colleague with a project or offering to make a valuable introduction.

The important thing is to approach every networking opportunity with the intention of giving first. This approach can open up new doors and create opportunities that you may never have considered before.

Another benefit of giving first is that it can lead to long-term success. When you establish a reputation as someone who is helpful and trustworthy, people are more likely to think of you when opportunities arise. They may recommend you for a job, introduce you to a valuable contact, or invite you to join a project.

In addition, when you give without expecting anything in return, you create a positive energy that can attract more opportunities and positive experiences into your life. People are drawn to positive energy and are more likely to want to be around someone who exudes it.

It is also important to remember that giving first does not mean giving away all your time and resources without regard for your own needs. It simply means approaching networking with the mindset of creating mutually beneficial relationships. You should still be strategic and intentional about the connections you make and the opportunities you pursue.

One way to approach networking with a giving mindset is to focus on the value you can provide to others. Instead of thinking about what you can get from someone, think about what you can offer them. This could be your expertise, your connections, your time, or your resources.

Another way to give in networking is to be genuinely interested in the people you meet. Ask them questions about their work, their interests, and their goals. Listen actively to their responses and look for ways to help them achieve their objectives. When you approach networking with a curiosity about others, you create a foundation for building strong, lasting relationships.

Summary Thoughts

1. Networking is a necessary skill for advancing in both business and career growth.

2. Networking involves creating connections and mutually rewarding relationships.

3. Successful networking involves giving value to others, not just taking from them.

4. Networking is not limited to extroverted individuals, and the real value lies in building long-term relationships based on trust and respect.

5. Giving first is crucial in networking, and it can lead to mutual benefits and long-term success.

6. Giving can take many forms, including introducing people, sharing information, volunteering time, and offering expertise.

7. A giving mindset in networking involves focusing on the value you can provide to others and being genuinely interested in their goals and interests.

8. Networking is an ongoing process that requires consistency, effort, and commitment.

9. The act of giving in networking creates a positive impression and builds trust with others, establishing a reputation as a valuable resource.

10. Giving without expecting anything in return creates positive energy and attracts more opportunities and positive experiences.

ACTIONABLE TAKEAWAYS JOURNAL

CHAPTER 3

THE GOLDEN RULE
OF NETWORKING

Let me now share what I consider to be the Golden Rule of Networking:

Give generously and generous gifts will be given back to you, shaken down to make room for more. Abundant gifts will pour out upon you with such an overflowing measure that it will run over the top! The measurement of your generosity becomes the measurement of your return.[10]

This "rule" is akin to the social psychology principle of reciprocity, which states that we tend to pay back what we received from others, in many social situations. This means if someone does you a favor, you tend to feel obligated to do something for the person in return. This is a human psychological hardwiring that we all obey by default, unless your conscience has become dysfunctional. So, smart people have learned to employ this principle to their advantage. I prefer to call it the Golden Rule of Networking though, given its essentiality for achieving results with strategic networking.

The first reason why smart people network is to give value. For them, it is always about value contribution. Smart people network because they have something to give; receiving comes secondary. Excellent networkers understand and appreciate the fact that when you network from a position of giving, you get stronger and almost indispensable. People appreciate you more and go out of their way to solve your needs when you have some. You easily win friends and expand your level of influence.

When you are willing to connect with people and give generously, the more people are willing to give to you. Anyone who understands networking for the purpose of giving and receiving value will go far in life. It is a cardinal principle, and every element of life honors it.

As the Golden Rule of Networking asserts, you receive generously when you give generously. When you give first—and generously—the universe is configured to reciprocate by bringing abundant, overflowing measures into your life. I particularly like the part that says, *"The measurement of your generosity becomes the measurement of your return."* If you have ever wondered why people who are smart at networking always give value to the people within their circles and seem to never lack opportunities and resources, this is your answer: they are obeying the Golden Rule of Networking. Do the same and you will enjoy those same results.

Wheel of Networking

The Wheel of Networking is a model I created based on more than two decades of studying, practicing, and reaping the dividends of strategic networking. It reveals the six cardinal qualities that make networking powerful and yielding. It encapsulates a principle, that if understood and imbibed, will both incite and empower anyone to deploy the vital skill that networking is.

Essentially, the Wheel of Networking has Giving at its center, being the heart of networking as we have explored already. Then, circling Giving are what I call the Five Cardinal Spokes. These are the valuable offers of strategic networking—what it does precisely to move your life forward when you engage in it.

As you know, a wheel is an instrument of both carriage and movement. Take a car wheel for example, it both carries the weight of the car and moves it from one place to another. Without wheels, a car will lose one of its core characteristic functions: mobility. Therefore, the Wheel of Networking is an instrument of progress in the practice of networking for results. So, having dealt with the heart of networking, which is Giving, let us now learn about the Five Cardinal Spokes.

Spoke 1: Ideas

One of the fundamental rewards of networking is that it creates room for idea sharing. People network because ideas are more valuable than precious metals in today's world, and they are highly mobile—constantly on the move. The speed at which ideas move in today's world is unprecedented. In fact, I believe that ideas don't reside in someone's mind alone—ideas visit and seek occupancy in many minds at the same time. They do so because they are eager to come to life. It appears as though ideas have grown weary of having many humans carry them to their graves after residing in their minds for decades, so they have re-strategized to nudging different people over time such that the person who takes action gets the win. Simply put, ideas have wings and fly at an incredible speed. So the more people you meet, the more ideas you are exposed to by way of interactional exchanges.

Exchanges of ideas is the reason some people travel to attend industry-specific or relevant social events. It will interest you to know that this practice is as old as the days of Aristotle, Socrates, Plato, and the other philosophers of ancient times. People traveled far distances to connect with other humans for purposes of sharing ideas and learning new things. There were public places that served as civic centers of some sort and dedicated to idea generation and exchanges. If you had a brilliant idea, say a new discovery, you were permitted to come into such spaces to meet and network with other people and share.

Many local and global businesses, institutions, and organizations today were built as a result of connecting with someone with a great idea, and with synergy the ideas evolved into products or services that are now serving mass markets and creating social good of varying scopes. This is why the advent of the internet ushered the world into an epoch of unprecedented fluidity of ideas, because the geographic boundaries were eliminated for good. People can connect virtually now; as a consequence of the resulting engagement and transaction, idea generation and implementation are growing at previously unimaginable levels. As you know, ideas lead to big opportunities. So, people network to exchange ideas.

Remember that ideas come formless, so even when you get an idea it may be unclear to you how best to tackle it for maximum benefits. But when you connect with the right people, there is an excellent chance that the idea will become clearer, placing you in a better position for implementing or scaling it. A simple comment by an expert, their explanation, a recommendation or referral might give you more insight into the idea. Again, this is one of the reasons people deliberately attend conferences. Beyond strategic socialization, it affords them opportunities for exchanging ideas. And of course, it is in exchanging ideas that bigger things are formed.

Notice that most people who have built sustainable companies today didn't build their companies on their own. For many of them, it was in the process of networking that they found like-minded people, people who shared an interest in the things they talked about. Therefore, networking is deliberate—and a vital necessity for success.

Spoke 2: Visibility

Another reason and reward of networking is getting to know more people and getting known by more people. Simply put, for visibility. If you are a person of value but your value is only known to your family members and friends, that is unfortunate and undermines your growth potential. Who lights a lamp and puts it under a table instead of on top of it? That would be the height of foolishness, wouldn't it? The purpose of a lamp is to light up a room, so having it under a table would limit the fulfillment of its purpose. This is what you do to yourself if you refuse to aggressively make yourself visible to your target audience.

There are people who need the value you represent, that you have. And they are often able and ready to pay for it, but if they don't know you they certainly wouldn't come to you. So what do you do? You take that value and go to the networking pitch with it. You get deliberate and active to know people and get known by them. Why? The more people you know and who know you in return, the more value or impact you can dispense—and the more you will get rewarded.

This is why good networkers define where they choose to go. They go where they can meet quality people and do what is called "social climbing." The more you know people, the more your network is enlarged, the more you can accomplish your goals, and the more money you can make—depending on the quality of the network. If you belong to a network and are finding it difficult to raise $10,000 in business capital, for example, you're better off without that network.

Nevertheless, there is a caveat. When you social climb, do so from a position of bringing quality value to the relationship. There must be something you bring to the table that the other person needs, so they can take it and return what you need. Remember the Golden Rule of Networking. Give value first and you will inevitably receive value in return.

Spoke 3: Credibility

Networking with the right person gives you credibility. One premium asset in business is trust. It is considered to be social capital, and with it you can draw so many other resources that could beat the imagination, including humungous sums of money.

When people trust you, they can do seemingly impossible things for you—even stake their reputation to make an opportunity work out for you. Trust is a powerful asset; never play light of it.

There are two basic ways to gain trust: earn it yourself or have it entrusted upon you. Follow me carefully. That was a tricky statement, but deliberate. At its root, trust is earned. When people meet you for the first time, they are mostly open-minded, expecting the best from you but having no guarantees of what they will get. Still, they hold on to the natural human faith that allows us to believe that a person we have just met will uphold their end of the bargain, whatever it is in that scenario. But as time passes, who we are unravels and determines whether the other person eventually trusts us or not. If you act in consistence with their expectations, they trust you. If not, they distrust you and keep you at arm's length. This is why and how trust is earned. It is earned by our actions, inactions, words, and attitude.

On the other hand, there is trust that is conferred. This is when another person places onto you their own reputation or trust level with a third person, often to grant you favor with the benefactor in that instance. This is why I said there are two ways to gain trust: you either earn it yourself or have it rubbed on you. The latter is the reason why you may hear someone say to a person he has just met, "You come highly recommended." That is conferred trust.

However, conferred trust is not enough. It is not sustainable for the long term; it is only temporary. Such trust is transient; it serves only to get you in the room—to give you access. Once access has been granted, you must now earn your own trust with the benefactor to ensure that the budding relationship continues for as long as possible, delivering optimal rewards for both of you.

Another reason for and reward of networking is that conferred trust gives you credibility. In fact, sometimes people may deal with you simply because someone significant is in your network, without that person necessarily recommending you. Why is that? Credibility. The logic is that if that significant person can trust you enough to deal with you, then you must be trustworthy, so you're given a chance. See how powerful strategic networking can be?

Spoke 4: Networks

The fourth Cardinal Spoke of the Wheel of Networking is strategically tapping into social networks for relevant areas of your life. As you can tell already, we all need to improve our social networks. The social network you belong to can determine how far you can go in a particular aspect of your life or in your career. That is why people deliberately join associations, institutes, professional affiliations, and religious bodies. Smart people join these networks for the purpose of meeting people and increasing their social networks. When you increase your social network, it impacts different areas of your life. It affords you to connect with people in your industry or a similar career path who may be able to open doors of growth opportunities for you. This is why people go out of their way to deliberately meet and network with people—for the purpose of business development or referrals.

Spoke 5: Relevance

The fifth Cardinal Spoke brings us back to where we started: Giving. In essence, we are saying here that networking gives you opportunities to showcase your relevance to a certain kind of people, market segment, community, and other areas. And of course, you need that exposure to elevate appreciation for your value and consequently drive demand for it. Everybody likes to associate with a relevant person, a person who doles out needed value in the exact measures required. That is an indispensable person to have in your network.

So as you showcase your relevance, what you will realize is that more people will be drawn to you, do business with you, and even refer you to their contacts, such that you will in turn be the one with whom people are desiring to connect. Now that is power! But it shouldn't pump you up pridefully, because if it does, you will repel people and lose the gains you had achieved. Stay humble and simple, yet strategic with your networking. Give value as often as you can and prove your relevance as a wholesome, valuable person. You will be an attractive force.

Case Study: Bringing It Home

When I was nearing graduation from high school, it dawned on me that my chances for a university education were bleak. My father was deceased, and my mother was taking care of nine children by herself. Going through high school had been a struggle, and further-ing my education wasn't in view. Where I come from, under such cir-cumstances a secondary education is considered a threshold, such that once I graduated my mother could take her attention off me and focus on getting my younger siblings to that threshold too.

In fact, the best I may have aspired to would have been enroll-ing in a school to learn a trade, and sooner or later be expected to start supporting the home. I knew the realities and the possibili-ties a trade provided, but I wanted more. I already had glimpses of what I wanted my future life to be about, and lacking a univer-sity education may have impeded the accomplishment of those goals. So, I sat down to think up a plan for getting what I wanted.

I wanted to attend the Government Secondary School in Owerri, Imo State, Nigeria, which happened to have a vibrant alumni community. So I went to the school and picked up the alumni directory and scanned through it to find who I could con-nect with for support toward my university education. I was armed with an important value that I knew one or two of them would appreciate—that I was the senior prefect of my class. Typically, being senior prefect meant you were well-rounded in a variety of values: academic, moral, attitude. It is a well-respected office in the school (I share how I became the senior prefect in my book, *Mind Leadership*). I decided to explore that course of action.

From the alumni directory, I made a list of 25 names to call, peo-ple who worked in great places. "Hello sir, my name is Linus Oko-rie. I just finished high school as captain of Government Secondary

School, Owerri. Can I come to visit you, sir?" I said to each of the 25 people over the phone. Interestingly, I received 20 nos and 5 yeses. I connected not asking for help immediately, but for them to know my name and a little about me.

The first of the five places I visited was in Warri, Delta State. The man I spoke with was the Regional Head of Environment, Africa, at Shell Petroleum Development Company, working at the Warri office. His family received me very warmly. I still recall that they drove me to their home in a Volkswagen Bora car and invited me stay with them for a few days. Thereafter, I became like their other son and was asked to visit them over some holidays during my university years.

Now here's an interesting part of this story. When I met the family, their youngest child was a little girl, while the other children were young boys in primary or secondary schools. Many years after, about 25 years, that girl traveled to school in the United States and graduated as the best student in accounting for her class. Later, my wife's younger brother, who is an accountant too and graduated with a first-class degree, had reason to travel to the US and I introduced them to each other. They connected and fell in love, quite remarkably. And as I write this, they are married and have two children.

What does this say? The rewards of networking can happen on a variety of fronts and levels. Networking can generate a multitude of possibilities. In this case, the family became helpful to me when I was attending the university, and later I was instrumental to their daughter meeting her life partner.

Another family I met during that strategic networking period was the Asolukas in Lagos, Nigeria. He accepted my request to meet with him. We became very close and they supported not only my education but my career so far. I have met many people while visiting Chief Asoluka's place, more than you can imagine, and many have been helpful to me one way or another. That means I was helped by the credibility of his network.

In addition, among the five families I networked with as a high school graduate, one was the managing director of a bank and became very helpful to my education by paying my school fees and giving me 30,000 naira for my upkeep every semester. Another one is presently the chairman of the board of directors at Guardians of the Nation (GOTNI) Leadership Center (the organization I lead) and ran for president of the Federal Republic of Nigeria for the 2023 elections. The same man gave me the opportunity to participate in the Nigeria Economic Summit a few years ago, when he was Chairman of the Nigerian Economic Summit Group. As you can imagine, he has given me several other opportunities to meet quality people.

So through strategic networking as a lad, I was able to not only attend and complete my university education, I gained an immeasurable push forward in life as well. Beyond that, these people provided me with mentorship, which is simply priceless and has coordinated my life toward becoming who I am privileged to be today.

Therefore, you network first to give value, then you receive value in return to aid your progress. In the process, networking can open doors for opportunities you may never have received otherwise.

Summary Thoughts

1. Networking is the art of creating connections and broadening your scope of influence, to the end of mutually rewarding gains.

2. Networking is a deliberate effort at meeting people, building relationships, sharing opportunities, and exchanging value.

3. In its truest essence, networking is an act undertaken by two or more parties with the intent to give and receive value.

4. When you are helpful, you compel the other person to be helpful to you. If you give value, the other person will feel impressed to return the gesture. It is like sowing a seed that will yield a harvest, all conditions being checked.

5. The first reason why smart people network is to give value. For them, it is always about value contribution. Smart people network because they have something to give; receiving comes secondary.

6. The Wheel of Networking is an instrument of progress in the practice of networking for results.

7. It appears as though ideas have grown weary of having many humans carry them to their graves after residing in their minds for decades, so they have re-strategized to nudging different people over time such that the person who takes action gets the win.

8. If you are a person of value but your value is only known to your family members and friends, that is unfortunate and undermines your growth potential.

9. The more you know people, the more your network is enlarged, the more you can accomplish your goals, and the more money you can make—depending on the quality of the network.

10. When people trust you, they can do seemingly impossible things for you—even stake their reputation to make an opportunity work out for you.

11. The rewards of networking can happen on a variety of fronts and levels. Networking can generate different possibilities.

ACTIONABLE TAKEAWAYS JOURNAL

CHAPTER 4

THE PORTRAIT AND ANATOMY OF A NETWORKING MAESTRO

The Man with the Golden Touch[11]

His career in media and television began with youth and good governance advocacy at the Nigeria Television Authority (NTA). As a passionate and vision-driven youngster, Adebola Williams (popularly called Debola Williams) worked at NTA for three years. That was where he connected with his future business partners, Chude Jideonwu and Late Emilia Asim-Ita, who also worked at NTA at the time. Together, they later founded Red Media Africa and The Future Awards.

As a young man, Williams gave himself to voluntary services whenever he saw an opportunity to fill. He committed himself to providing solutions to problems as a way of giving back to society as well as building quality networks, a currency he understood quite well from a young age.

From the start of their business, instead of being driven by profits, Williams and his partners were focused on finding resources as well as generating value to meet people's needs. Having set their priorities and vision right, they linked up with a lawyer, Godswill Osako, who doubled as their company's lawyer for seven years at no cost. Osako gave the duo an office space at Sabo Yaba in Lagos to serve as their office. In return, they gave him value in various ways, some of which included Jideonwu writing articles and providing some secretarial assistance for him. Godswill Osako believed in them because he saw their passion, grit, relentless spirit, and commitment to what they had set out to do. This helped to build a strong relationship between them, and over time led to sharing mutually rewarding contacts.

Furthermore, to grow and expand the scope and profitability of their business, the duo focused on leveraging the human currency. They achieved this by deliberately cultivating a rich network through various means, including providing pro bono services, sending gifts, and generally meeting, maintaining, and sustaining quality relationships with people.

Debola Williams believed his greatest investment to be people. And because they built their business organically, they focused on people for growth and sustenance. They built worth and trust with people who in turn provided the network they needed for growth and expansion. The other people, on the other hand, were convinced that their investment in the young founders was ideal, as they saw their vigor, resilience, commitment, and readiness to work.

Williams and Jideonwu also developed an earn-as-you-sell percentage model for their company. This meant that anyone who brought business received a commission, which became a strategic incentive that helped drive growth, as each staff became a marketer for the company. This implied that each staff had to work at developing their network and building quality relationships. Consequently, the duo cultivated significant relationships over time that later helped propel Williams beyond Nigeria and into the rest of Africa.

Today, Debola Williams, born in 1986, is a media mogul, journalist, political consultant, and motivational speaker. He is the CEO of Red Africa Group, Africa's largest portfolio of young media companies, including Red Media Africa, Statecraft Inc., The Future Awards Africa, and YNaija; cofounded with Chude Jideonwu. Williams was recognized by *Forbes* as the man who helped to elect a trifecta of presidents in Africa and was dubbed "the man with the golden touch" by Ghanaian President Nana Akufo-Addo.[12] This christening is a consequence of his help that saw the opposition candidate winning against the incumbent president on his third attempt in 2016. He did the same in Nigeria when in 2015 he led the rebranding of Nigeria's current president, Muhammadu Buhari, using media engagement to shift long-held perceptions and impact elections.

As a result, Williams now consults in several African countries. His success in numerous political arenas has tremendously bolstered his networks and ties, which now extend across the African conti-nent.[13] This has made Williams a dependable and effective political counsel across several African countries, particularly through his governance communications expression, Statecraft Inc. This is in addition to diverse global recognitions that he has acquired, along-side membership in numerous bodies serving for social good.

One of Debola Williams's pleasurable acts has always been giv-ing gifts to people, especially during festive seasons or special dates in their lives. This strategy has helped him grow his net-work by inadvertently endearing him to his beneficiaries—owing to the Golden Rule of Networking. More than his giving, Debola Williams is known to be deliberate at introducing himself to pol-iticians and influential persons whenever he attends events. He walks up to his target, greets them, and introduces himself, mak-ing sure to comment on something good and impressive about the person's work before leaving them with his business card. This calculated move, almost more than anything else, has been pivotal in expanding his network.

The Portrait

From the foregoing story, it is apparent that Debola Williams is adept at networking. It is a weapon he has masterfully wielded throughout his professional life and continues to wield. And of course, he is not alone. Networking is the weapon of the great, no matter where they are in the world. It is what highly successful people use to rise above pedestrian achievements.

Now, let us x-ray who a networking maestro is. Who is a net-worker? What are their qualities? What do they look like? What are their character traits and how can anyone interested enough develop them? This is the thrust of this chapter. But before we delve in fully, let us consider the portrait of a master in the art of networking.

The Merriam-Webster Dictionary defines the word "portrait" as "a pictorial representation of a person usually showing the face." So, here we want to see what the "face" of a networker looks like. When you meet a masterful networker, what should you expect to "see" by default? Simply, it is *capacity for value*. Capacity for value is the master key for strategic networking.

To elucidate, let me draw your mind back to the Golden Rule of Networking. Recall that we established that true networking is founded and thrives on the premise of giving. Therefore, your capacity for churning and delivering qualitative, useful value is the determinant of how good you are as a networker.

This is the logic: no person of value keeps company with a parasite, someone who comes only to take from them. Masterful networkers understand the reciprocity principle, the Golden Rule of Networking, and are committed to upholding it. So when they meet anyone who abuses the rule, they instantly disconnect from that person. They approach every new connection from the stance of giving and expecting value, and they expect the other person to come the same way too. If you lack the capacity for value, you are of little or no worth to them, so they drop you. And lest you take offense at this, it is a subconscious human tendency, although hinged on the understanding of the Golden Rule of Networking. That means if in their shoes, you would do the same thing.

Therefore, if you are ever looking for a person who can ace networking, all other factors being constant, look for a person with a rich *capacity for value*. That is your person. And if you want to employ the power of networking to push your life forward, be that type of person. Develop your capacity for value. Give generously and you will receive generously, so says the Golden Rule of Networking.

The Anatomy

Driving our conversation further, having now seen the "face" of a networking maestro, what does his internal side look like? What is he made of? What qualities define him? What drives him toward being a master at networking? Eight qualities lead to becoming a networking maestro: 1) Outgoing; 2) Sincere; 3) Friendly; 4) Good Listener; 5) Proactive; 6) Trustworthy; 7) Empathetic; 8) Appreciative.

1. Outgoing

First, it is important for a networker to be outgoing. You must learn the fact that everything you need to make progress in life is in someone's pocket or another's contact list. Someone has the money, connection, ideas, relationships, etc. that you need, so your ability to leave where you are and get out to engage with people is important. The person who wants to network robustly must be outgoing, even if you are an introvert. You must get out of your comfort zone. Also know that networking can happen in the most unlikely places, but surely out of your house. So, go out often.

When you meet someone at the airport, don't wait for the person to introduce him or herself—you should extend an introduction first. I cannot count how many times my outgoing disposition has put food in my mouth, figuratively speaking. I've met several people just passing by and I had to stop to introduce myself. You want to be a great person and yet you don't know even one person who lives on the same street with you? And don't tell me you are shy, you're not a "people person," or you don't know how to strike up a conversation. You may think those are valid reasons, but they are not—they are *excuses*.

Networking is deliberate. Realizing its enormous power to impact your life, you must develop the capacity to deliberately get out, and your intention to connect with people must be clear. Don't be comfortable with being an introvert. Your temperament should be a resource to serve your growth, not limit you.

I remember a time I deliberately went out of my way to reach out to MTN Nigeria Communications. I wanted sponsorship for a GOTNI Leadership Program and someone informed me that MTN awarded a lot of sponsorships. I reached out to them and connected with one of the management members who advised me how to penetrate effectively for the result I was seeking. In the space of a few weeks, I attended their events and connected with more people, eventually leading to a grant for the program. Interestingly, every major grant I have received for Guardian of the Nation International (GOTNI) Leadership Center was through knowing someone inside the respective organizations.

As another example, one time I attended a dinner event organized by the Central Bank of Nigeria (CBN). The CBN was hosting the Princess of Netherlands and a friend invited me. I went with copies of my book and my complementary cards, deliberate to network. There, I met a director at CBN, introduced myself, and handed him a copy of my book. Much to my wonder, he expressed shock that I published a book with my photo on the cover. He said he had never been to a bookshop overseas and saw a Nigerian author on the cover of their book. He was vividly impressed.

"What do you do?" he asked.

"I'm a leadership coach and I teach for a living; we train institutional leaders," I told him.

"Wow! Let's negotiate. I am planning a retreat for my department. It'll be at Akwanga, Nasarawa State. I have invited someone from South Africa who would lead the leadership session, but I will bring you along. How much will you charge?"

I told him my fee and he agreed right there.

After I delivered my session at the retreat, I somewhat became the main speaker because I blew their minds away. Then they bought all the copies of my books I had brought along with me. How did it all start? It was my outgoing nature that made that possible. And this is only one of several instances where just reaching out to network brought good value to me.

2. Sincere

I have discovered that many people want to network, but their intentions are not sincere. They have an ulterior motive in their heart about meeting people. They connect to get something. They size up people before attempting to make a connection. This is not a good thing to do. In fact, it is the reason many people don't get desirable results, because they approach networking from a selfish angle. Whereas, networking should be about genuine exchange of value.

I remember one day I was at Transcorp Hilton in Abuja for a haircut. When I was ready to leave, I saw a man standing by who was somewhat casually dressed, but I had respect for him still. And being my usual self, I connected with him and we exchanged cards. Strangely, I didn't look at his card after he handed it to me; I simply went on to attend to the concern on my mind. When I came back, he had left. Then the barber asked me, "Do you know who you just met?" A little taken aback by the question, I answered no while reaching for the card in my pocket. I was pleasantly surprised; the man was occupying a very powerful position in Nigeria. The next time we met was in his office, and it has been over 8 years of valuable exchanges worth significant financial fortunes.

Notice that the edge I had here was sincerity of heart. I didn't reach out to him because I thought he was someone I could get something from, I reached out because it was proper. Networking has no time or season; it is something we can do anytime, anywhere, whenever. Remember, people want to feel that you are real and authentic before they open up to you. So, be sincere.

Another case in point was a woman I met in Dallas, Texas, in 2015. At a conference, I was honored by Dr. George Fraser, based on the work I've done and continue to do in Africa. Alongside receiving the award, I was requested to give a speech to address the conference audience that gathered more than 2,000 highly successful African Americans. Gratefully, the audience was quite thrilled by my speech and gave me a standing ovation when I was finished. Then several people wanted to meet with me for brief chats, introductions, and compliments when the event closed.

Interestingly, a woman approached me and communicated a different vibe from everyone else. The first thing she said was that she was proud to be African. That instantly caught me. That was different from everything I'd heard till that moment. More so, I could see and feel the sincerity in her words, energy, and remarks. I could sense it was all coming from a pure place. She was sincere. No pretense or ambiguity. She went on say that I had inspired her and she wanted to know how she could help me push my work within the United States of America. She was practically offering to help me succeed in the USA. She asked how she could make my stay and work in America thrive—perhaps facilitate my meeting or connection with people important to my work. Simply, she made that conversation not about her but about me. And because she did that, I naturally opened up and we connected meaningfully. Now she is one of my partners in the US and is quite involved with my work in the country—ever since that meeting.

Sincerity is a key component of networking. You must come to the networking table with a heart that is sincere. Don't compliment someone if it isn't coming from your heart. That is not networking; that is manipulation, and the conscientious person can sense it. Don't try to manipulate people. To access people's hearts, you have to be sincere. You have to be sincere in your words, compliments, approach, conversation, everything. You have to be sincere in your motive.

Unfortunately, there are a lot of people whose motives lack integrity. I'm talking about why you want to meet or connect with this person. Are you genuinely interested in the person? Are you genuinely interested in connecting for the purpose of exchanging qualitative value? Come to the networking table with sincerity. Otherwise, stay away for good. You are better off wherever else you'll be.

3. Friendly

Have you ever met a person who wasn't friendly? Great friends must show themselves friendly. It is a rule of thumb. You cannot approach people in an attempt to connect with them and hold your face like a flint rock. Your attempt is as good as dead on arrival. You must exude warmth and a friendly demeanor. And it works both ways, whether you are approaching or being approached. Be warm and friendly.

When I contested for governorship in Imo State, Nigeria, in 2019, I was always smiling at everyone. I am the kind of person who once you smile at me, I want to hug you. So the security team had to warn me against that disposition in the political space. They advised me to curtail my friendliness because of the potential for danger at the time. Understanding the import of their advice, I had to comply, but it was difficult for me.

People respect warmth. The smile you generate is effective. When you meet people for the first time and you are friendly, they want to meet you again. But if you meet people and you are frowning, they will avoid you. So what usually happens in networking settings is that people dodge people whose nonverbal communication is reading unfriendly. Take my word for it.

One thing you must bear in mind is that people are different. Every human being is a complex being. So, appreciate the fact that there's complexity already in place whenever you are seeking to network with someone new.

For an introvert, that means it is your responsibility to work on yourself to get better at networking, by learning how to engage and interact with diverse types of people. It is true that, because every human being is different, some people's default disposition does not show friendliness. If you are such a person, know that others will not be attracted to you when you don't have a friendly demeanor.

Therefore, one of the greatest strengths of a networker is the ability to cultivate a personality that is attractive, a personality that is friendly. This means that if you meet somebody in an elevator, for example, instead of waiting to be greeted, you can smile and say, "Great morning. It's nice to meet you. I'm...." Show yourself as friendly. No doubt in some cases people will reject or ignore you, but it doesn't matter. In fact, in most cases people will respond with a smile and exchange a pleasantry or two with you, which could be the spark of a great relationship—you never know.

Again, be willing and disposed to being friendly. Open up and connect with people genuinely. And let me tell you, because leaders are dealers in hope, the positive energy a friendly person emits makes a big difference in people's lives most times. That is what compels them to reciprocate the gesture and open up to connect.

4. Great Listener

To ace networking, be a great listener. Talkers are many, listeners are few. Making yourself a listener will instantly distinguish you and project you as a likable person to connect with. When you meet someone for the first time, don't talk too much; instead, listen more and do the asking.

Funnily, I have found that many people do weird things when they meet a rich person. The most disturbing one is when they start speaking the language of poverty by asking for favors. What they fail to know is that rich people are tired of liabilities.

They are tired of people bothering them with requests, so they disconnect from them immediately if they speak that language. Don't join that band of foolishness. When you meet someone for the first time, especially one more accomplished than you are, listen and ask questions. This singles you out in their mind, giving you an edge over everyone else.

This is one of my strategies. When I meet with people who are of better placement than I have, I behave like I know nothing and ask as much questions as time and the scenario allow. There was a time I met the CEO of a major transport company in Nigeria, with ventures in other African countries as well—a billionaire. Though accomplished in his own right, he has set up structures that enable him to be a support system for a lot of disadvantaged people. So I asked him questions and listened to the valuable insights he shared so generously.

We met onboard a flight and talked all through, so much that we continued to talk as we walked off the plane and into the terminal. Why? Most accomplished people have so much to talk about, a lot of wisdom to dispense, but there is often only a little demand to hear what they have to share. Usually when people meet successful people, they want to talk about their own accomplishments. This is wrong! Why would they talk about their own accomplishments to someone who is obviously many times more accomplished?

I urge you to listen and seize the chance to learn. Talking too much is exactly how to make a poor impression, whereas listening and asking questions is how to stay in a person's mind and establish a good relationship. The moment you become a great listener, you become valuable to people. And of course, people like to go where there is value.

5. Proactive

A networker must be proactive. Being proactive is the ability to make creative and actionable decisions on your feet. This means seizing networking opportunities on the spot, as occasions present. It means going into a place and proactively engaging with a valuable person on the spur of the moment. Don't be in an environment where there are quality people and you keep quiet. That is business or professional suicide. That is losing opportunities you may never even know you missed. It is all about knowing the right timing and seizing the chance as it shows up, on demand. It also requires the skilled ability to observe people's mood and make prompt decisions when they are in their best mood. Proactivity is rightly positioning yourself and taking the right steps to engage with people who may prove valuable in the near or distant future.

More often than not, great connections that later proved highly valuable were not planned. The people involved were just in the right environment at the time and one or both of took proactive steps. You might attend a meeting where you never expected someone to show up, but because you are proactive you already know what to do to seize the moment.

By the way, I encourage you to make a list of the people you want to meet before going to a meeting or conference. The deliberate act of taking steps to research people who will be at any gathering is proactiveness. The lasting bond is created by the things you say to the people you meet. That is what determines whether they will give you their attention and possibly their business card or not. This is especially powerful when you say something complimentary of their work or impact in society. People love such gestures.

For instance, if you meet someone and say, "Sir, I listened to your interview three days ago on …and it answered a nagging question I have had for a long time. Thank you very much." That is more than enough to get the person's attention. They would most likely thank you for the compliment, then ask what question it was that you had and what they said in particular that answered that question for you. Before you realize it, you both could be having a hearty and cheerful conversation, which more than likely will create room for subsequent engagements. I have met several people that way—what I knew about them was my key to latching onto the opportunity.

You will never get some people's attention if you don't create a reference point. It could be as simple as you went to the same school, belong to the same club or association somewhere, things like that. There are other avenues, of course; these are only examples. There are multiple ways you can strike up an engaging conversation and connect with people. Your ability to be proactive, to research and know the right things to say, and the right time to connect with them can make a difference for you. You must take action again and again and again. Be proactive when you must. Take advantage of every opportunity, some don't come often.

6. Trustworthy

We have dealt much with the importance of trust, so I won't repeat. Simply, being trustworthy means developing an appealing reputation. Imagine if you met someone and they quickly did a background check on you. They find good commendations about you, which becomes an instant validation and access for you. So, for a networker, a good reputation is a plus. It spells that your person or brand can be trusted. It opens doors for you.

7. Empathetic

One of the worst things you can do to yourself is talk poorly to someone about someone else. You may think you are eliciting sympathy, but in reality you are shooting yourself in the foot. By default, the person thinks, *If he speaks so poorly about someone else to me, he would surely speak about me this way to another person. I don't want that, so I'll stay away!*

Another scenario. While you are talking with someone in your office, you receive a call from one of your staff reporting that he is sick and won't be in the office today. The way you respond to that call will show whether you are an empathetic person or not, and creating either a favorable or unfavorable perception of you in the person you are talking with.

Third scenario: Your spouse calls you and just before taking the call you quip irritatingly, "What a pain in the neck; always calling and interrupting me!" If the person you're talking to loves his or her spouse, what do you suppose will happen? The person will think, *This is bad company, I'm going to stay away.*

These are bad attitudes we often express almost unconsciously, and they sabotage our networking efforts. Unfortunately, many people exhibit these behaviors. So when you deal with someone and an unpleasant situation arises, the way you deal with it can determine whether the person decides to take things to the next level with you or not. Empathy is a human virtue, get some. So many people have lost great networks because of poor, empathy-starved attitudes.

8. Appreciative

Another core component every networker must have is forwardness to appreciate people. Great networkers are very deliberate and keen on appreciating people, even when they have just met the person. They readily use words such as, "I'm honored to meet you," "I appreciate meeting you," "Thank you for your time." They show this in their attitude and in how they present themselves.

The business of networking is my life. It is what I do daily. I can tell you for free that this strategy works wonders. Never act as though you have a right to people's time or attention. It's a gift and it should be treated as such. Value the gift of their time and interest in talking with you and thank them for it. That is how to consolidate whatever positive impression you may have made on them.

I just gave you another secret weapon. If you disregard it, it will be to your disadvantage.

Summary Thoughts

1. Networking is essential to achieve success in any field or industry.

2. A successful networking maestro possesses a rich capacity for value and abides by the Golden Rule of Networking.

3. To become a networking maestro, it's important to have eight essential qualities – outgoing, sincere, friendly, a good listener, proactive, trustworthy, empathetic, and appreciative.

4. To network effectively, one must be willing to step outside their comfort zone and engage with people in diverse settings.

5. Sincerity, friendliness, and active listening are the key ingredients of successful networking.

6. Setting clear intentions and goals can help networkers focus their efforts and achieve specific results.

7. A positive attitude and friendly demeanor can go a long way in creating strong and lasting connections.

8. Successful networking requires proactivity, trust-worthiness, empathy, and appreciation, which are crucial components of building meaningful relationships with others.

ACTIONABLE TAKEAWAYS JOURNAL

CHAPTER 5

NETWORKING THE RIGHT WAY

Now armed with both the "portrait" and the "anatomy" of an expert networker, let's explore the correct way to network for results in today's world. Remember that this 21st century is a world so fast paced that keeping up with the flow is nearly a tall order. It is a world with no precedence. Yet, we must make every effort to thrive and succeed at our endeavors, to make an indelible impact on as many people and systems as possible. As we have established so far, the right way is to leverage the awesome power of strategic networking. But how exactly should you network today to get the maximum possible results? The following are nine ways to do just that:

1. Start with a goal.
2. Always carry your business cards.
3. Practice power introduction.
4. Utilize every moment.

5. Deliberately join organizations.

6. Give ideas, referrals, and gestures.

7. Organize your networking assets.

8. Promote your value.

9. Make the first contact.

Now let's look at each one in more detail.

1. Start With a Goal

The first thing to do is to set a goal for how many people you want to meet per year, quarter, month, or event. Yes, goal setting applies in networking too, so prioritize it. And don't just set the target number, also set a preferred, workable schedule for achieving it. Set a tenure for the target number of new connections to be met. It could be monthly or yearly, or even weekly.

This will help you to achieve two things. First, it will keep you focused and agile, determined to meet your target. Second, it will culture your mind to be creative and advise you on ways to accomplish the goal. It will also make you proactive in those unplanned moments we talked about earlier where you meet people unexpectedly. Because you are working toward a defined mark, your mind will be on edge to spot opportunities for quality networking. And where it doesn't find, it will create and propose to you for creative actions. Therein lies the power of goal setting in networking, much like in every other area of our lives.

Never go to any event without setting a goal. Imagine that you attend three events every week and connect with five people at each, by the end of each week you would have met fifteen people in total. In a month, you would have sixty new contacts in your network. How powerful is that! If you keep at it and also apply the different principles and tips we have learned so far and will further share as we progress, how possible is it that you will ever lack vital resources for accomplishing your dreams and ambitions?

So, deliberately attend as many events as possible that embody your passions, profession, and/or business interests. And before you wonder where or how you will find events to attend, you don't know about them because you are not searching for them. There are always events happening. Also, you don't have to be invited before you can attend; seek out events with open access and attend. The only ones to avoid are those with the "strictly by invitation" tag. There are several online platforms that showcase upcoming events, even social media; start there.

2. Always Carry Your Business Cards

Don't just attend events, carry your business cards with you at all times. Here's a rule of thumb: You don't deserve to collect another person's business card without giving yours. It is even worse to write your phone number for a new connection on a piece of paper. That is poor image projection, bad first impression. Oh, there is the new trend of calling out your phone number while the other person types it on their phone; that is poor too, don't do it.

The professional way to exchange contacts with a new connection and keep your mutual respect intact is to exchange business cards. This is very important, yet commonly flouted. To easily distinguish yourself, practice this religiously—simple as it appears.

If you meet someone who is about to catch a flight, would you have them pause so you can write your phone number on a piece of paper (if you find one, that is)? Or would you delay them just so they can type out your phone number on their phone? It is clumsy and time-wasting. Exchanging cards is the effective way.

3. Practice Power Introduction

Even when you have your business card with you, you must be able to introduce yourself effectively. It is called "power introduction." This is introducing yourself in a compelling manner that makes the other person want to hear what you have to say further. It is commonly called an "elevator pitch."

An elevator pitch is a concise and persuasive speech intended to spark a person's attention and interest in you and what you do. Usually, you say an elevator pitch when you meet someone for the first time and move to connect with them. And ideally, it should be said in 30 seconds, preferably less. Also, if your pitch is strong and powerful enough, it should initiate a conversation between you and the target, largely because it should end with a call to action that could mean the person asking a follow-up or clarifying question. That sets the tone and gets you both conversing productively—hopefully.

Your power introduction should include your name, followed by a complimentary remark about the other person. Next, say what you do for a living as well as how it relates or can apply to the person's work. Then close with a question that invites him or her to respond. That way, the person has a fair idea of what you do and can picture what is the common ground between you two, which becomes the basis for a conversation.

Another thing to note is that many times it is best to wait for the person to request your card. But we mostly flout it, perhaps for fear of losing out if they eventually don't ask for it. However, if your introduction is powerful enough and you have a productive conversation, people will often ask for your card. Great networkers provide their 30-second power speech and wait for their cards to be requested.

4. Utilize Every Moment

There must be preparation before you can succeed at networking. To be successful in your quest to network, you need to know in advance what to do before you meet the people. In simple terms, preparation precedes networking.

Always mingle and meet with people before an event starts, during breaks, and after the event. You are there largely to build up your network, aren't you? So why waste any moment?

One of the things brilliant networkers do is arrive early for events. They understand that latecomers miss a significant chunk of the networking pie. So they get in early and get to work. Then they craftily use the lunch break to network some more. And after every event, they spare some more minutes to close out their business for the day. Do likewise.

5. Deliberately Join Organizations

Join communities and get involved with their activities, whether by membership or volunteerism. This is such a powerful principle that most people neglect, yet it has immense potential to push you forward if you engage it. The reason is that most communities are levelers in that they assemble people of varying societal cadres in one place, allowing you to easily reach people you may otherwise not meet outside that space. Therefore, deliberately identify and join associations and groups where there are opportunities to meet people. The more associations you belong to, the more networking opportunities you will have. Memberships and volunteerism can help you to grow your network almost more than anything else.

6. Give Ideas, Referrals, and Gestures

Let me again refer you to the Golden Rule of Networking. Recall it is about giving first before expecting to receive. So, give ideas, referrals, and any gestures that the other person would find helpful. Yes, learn how to give to people out of your own volition or whenever you find a need in their life. Sometimes it could be as simple as offering to pay for someone's meal at a restaurant. I have experienced goodwill through this too. I have had times when I have offered to pay for meals and the gesture landed me some opportunities.

You must be a promoter of other people. That is today's way to network. When you meet someone who compliments a third party, that person is a great networker. Always speak good things about other people and be quick to refer them whenever you find an opportunity that matches their competence. Most well-accomplished people today have a reputation of connecting people to growth opportunities.

7. Organize Your Networking Assets

One mistake many people make is failing to harness their networking assets. This means aggregating and organizing all the business cards you have ever collected. Do this from time to time to keep yourself abreast of the contacts you have and follow up with them. In other words, learn to organize and keep in touch with your current network. This way you can easily reach out to people, feel their advancement pulse, and stay top-of-mind so that no opportunities pass you by.

As a starter rule, whenever you meet someone for the first time, the next call from you should never be to ask for favors. If you do that, you are abusing your network. The procedure is to send a text message telling them how pleased you were to meet them, and you look forward to meeting them again. Most times they will reply with the same or similar response and the relationship kickstarts.

8. Promote Your Value

Another principle is to strategically advertise yourself, the value you bring to the marketplace. Every time you network is an opportunity for you to showcase the value you bring to the table. The marketplace is interested in and thrives on value creation and distribution. Once you advertise the value you represent, people who share similar interests with you or need that value will be happy to connect with you.

Another technique is to develop yourself so much that you're not always the one trying to meet people. Make yourself so valuable and attractive that others can desire, even aspire, to meet with you. I was one time at a public event where a police officer in uniform and holding a gun saw me and hurried to heartily hug me, him and his gun together. I remember that my shirt got a little stained in the process, but it didn't matter; I was touched by the frantic gesture. He said I had impacted his life very much by adding value to him, and he was happy to meet me in person. It was almost a reflex action, and I was grateful that my life has created so much value that someone could go out of the protocol of his job to show me his appreciation. It was heartwarming. Also, such moments can be a premise for networking. As the person is excitedly talking about your impact in their lives, there may be someone listening and could become so impressed as to offer you an opportunity. What goes around, comes around.

9. Make the First Contact

I always advise people not to wait for people to connect with you; rather, you need to make the first contact. Be the first to make the connection. But feel at liberty to disconnect when the person says something you can't relate with or provides no real value. This is important because, as you may know, opportunities come very disguised, so waiting for the other person to connect may mean missing out on an opportunity that could transform your life remarkably. The following is a case in point.

One day a long time ago, I was sitting by myself having a drink at one of Abuja's prestigious hotels. I noticed a man sitting by himself nearby. Although the man was dressed in a suit, I could tell he was from the northern part of the country. Of course, I have learned to never disregard any such opportunities, so I went over and talked with him. I introduced myself first, and during our conversation I shared the vision of GOTNI with him.

He was very impressed with my work and said he had someone I must meet. It turned out to be the MD/CEO of a renowned commercial bank. Just like that, he gave me access to the man, who also took a liking to me when we met. Believe me when I say the story of my life took a complete positive twist from that point forward. That contact made a huge difference for me. That MD became one of the key funders of my major projects for eight consecutive years. He even funded some of my personal development training overseas. All this happened because I reached out. In fact, I can't talk about GOTNI without talking about this man. The impact was profound!

Summary Thoughts

1. Networking is the weapon of the great, no matter where they are in the world. Networking is what highly successful people use to rise above pedestrian achievements.

2. Your capacity for churning and delivering qualitative, useful value is the determinant of how well of a networker you are.

3. Don't be comfortable with being an introvert. Your temperament should be a resource to serve your growth, not limit you.

4. Networking has no time or season; we can network anytime, anywhere, whenever. People want to feel that you are real and authentic before they open up to you.

5. Come to the networking table with sincerity. Otherwise, stay away for good.

6. Talkers are many, listeners are few. Making yourself a listener instantly distinguishes you and projects you as a likable person with whom to connect.

7. Don't be in an environment where there are quality people and you keep quiet. That is business or professional suicide.

8. Empathy is a human virtue, get some. So many people have lost great networks because of poor, empathy-starved attitudes.

9. Never act as though you own a right to people's time or attention. It's a gift and it should be treated as such. Value the gift of their time and interest in talking with you and thank them for it.

10. A rule of thumb: You don't deserve to collect another person's business card without giving yours.

11. When you meet someone who compliments a third party, that person is a great networker. Always speak good things about other people and be quick to refer them whenever you find an opportunity that matches their competence.

12. The marketplace is interested in and thrives on value creation and distribution. Once you advertise the value you represent, people who share similar interests with you or need that value will be happy to connect with you.

ACTIONABLE TAKEAWAYS JOURNAL

CHAPTER 6

GENERAL RULES OF NETWORKING

The Happenstance That Redefined Giving

Something you may have sensed as a silent undertone in our discourse so far is the fact that many times networking happens in very unlikely manners and later brings about results that may never have been foreseen. This is precisely what happened with billionaires Warren Buffett and Bill Gates. Theirs was an unlikely connection that would later rock the world in many wonderful ways.

On July 5, 1991, when Bill Gate's mother invited him to attend a meeting where Warren Buffett would be, he was rather unenthusiastic about meeting Buffett and decidedly uncooperative. To Gates, Buffett didn't do much except pore over papers trying to guess the direction of the stock market, so he felt they had nothing in common and would have nothing to talk about. Well, Bill's mother prevailed on him and he reluctantly attended the meeting, promising to spend just an hour. Buffett was also apprehensive about not having anything in common with Gates. When they met and began a conversation, however, they ended up spending the entire day together, and left promising to meet up again.[14]

This started a rewarding relationship between Warren Buffett and Bill and Melinda Gates, which solidified into the creation of The Giving Pledge decades later. This pledge is a promise made by billionaires around the world to give a significant portion of their wealth to charitable causes, either during their lifetime or in their will. This singular act of connecting billionaire business people worldwide to give back to society has proven to be a record-breaking move that shows just how effective a tool of change and dynamic progress networking is. According to *The Wall Street Journal*, as of December 2021, The Giving Pledge has more than 230 wealthy people from 28 countries who have pledged portions of their wealth to social good.[15]

After developing a fine relationship with many personal and business gains through the years, not minding the fact that there exists almost three decades of age difference between the two billionaires, the Gates' founded the Bill & Melinda Gates Foundation in 2000. Then they partnered with Warren Buffett to found The Giving Pledge in 2010. And though a shrewd businessman, Warren Buffett donated over 85 percent of his wealth to the Gates Foundation. This was the first time in history that a man of his repute and wealth chose not to establish a charity in his own name, but rather donate almost his entire wealth to another foundation. For a man worth $110.4 billion (as of January 17, 2023),[16] we know that was huge! Again, the power of networking!

From Networking to Leading a Corporation

Another story showing the power of networking is that of Warren Buffett and Gregory Edward Abel. On May 1, 2021, executive vice chair of Berkshire Hathaway, Charlie Munger, made a seemingly passive comment at the corporation's annual shareholder meeting indicating Gregory Abel, vice chair of Non-Insurance Business Operations, as Berkshire Hathaway's successor CEO. Warren Buffett confirmed this on CNBC two days later.

Now here's the interesting part. Abel first got on Buffett's radar through a mutual friend of theirs, Walter Scott, who spoke highly of him. Perhaps owing to the recommendation and due diligence, a year later, in 2000, Berkshire Hathaway acquired MidAmerican Energy Holdings that Abel was running at the time. Since then, Greg Abel has been at Berkshire Hathaway Energy and making giant strides, which earned him the tag of being a low-key but hardworking dealmaker, having spearheaded some of Berkshire's biggest and most successful acquisitions. Decades into the future, since they first connected in 1999, Abel has been tapped to become the CEO of the multibillion-dollar company.[17]

Networking Is Dynamic Power

It is to your detriment if you neglect or disregard networking. As you can see from the foregoing stories, networking is planting a seed today that could yield unimaginable fruits in the future. Networking is laying the foundation for a prosperous future for yourself and the people you love. With strategic networking, you can set the tone of what kind of tomorrow you want to have. And not only for you, but for your descendants as well.

I heard the brief story of a Nigerian thought leader. He is mid-aged and has done tremendous work to impact many lives, young and not-so-young alike. One day, a protégé came to him with a significant financial gift as appreciation for the man's impact on his growth. Politely, he thanked his protégé but declined taking the gift. Rather, he said to the young man, "My son is very young and I may not be around very long into when his future will be starting out in earnest, so I am making a list of people to gift my son when he turns 18. These are people who give me their word that if my son ever calls them for help, they will answer him. I would like to add your name to the list if you agree." Of course, the young man agreed, owing to the qualitative impact he had received from his mentor. That is strategic networking for future harvest!

Networking is like making deposits in a futuristic, invisible bank account that you can make big withdrawals from on demand. These deposits will likely serve to give your life big forward leaps. However, you can never tell what exactly the harvest will be; all you know for sure is that there is a high chance of quality withdrawals.

Now, what are the playbook rules for networking correctly and positioning to maximize each connection? How do you make networking work for you and push you forward? There are six rules to ad here to:

1. Ask Questions, Then Listen

I spoke about this in the previous chapter, but it is worth stating here again. It is an all-too-common error. Most people are too eager to talk about themselves when they meet new people. That is the bandwagon effect at play. Most feel that is the right approach because networking has been sold to us as a medium of marketing our products or services. That is true, but half-baked. I encourage you to try my recommendation: The next time you meet and are networking with someone new, especially if the person is more advanced in accomplishments than you are, ask questions, then stop talking and listen. Let the other person do more of the talking. This will immediately distinguish you from the pack and earn you a seat in their mind.

Accomplished people know so much from personal experience and study, and many wish to share as much as possible so as to help people avoid the pitfalls. Yet very few people ask for their insights. Therefore, when they find anyone who creates room for them to share their wisdom, they are happy to respond with generosity.

Again, don't talk about yourself when you meet new people, ask a lot of questions, and listen more. Give a power introduction as stated before, then guide the conversation to allow them to talk. Take a cue from yourself; you like to talk about yourself, so do others. If you therefore apply the wisdom of allowing the other person to talk about themselves more, they will almost instantly like you. That is a power trick; use it!

2. Keep in Touch

How many people have you connected with in the past but have not spoken to in the past three to five years? Why is it important to keep in touch? I'll answer that question with my own mistake in this regard.

I met Nigeria's current vice president, Professor Yemi Osinbajo, two days before he was announced as the running mate for President Muhammadu Buhari. We met at Transcorp Hilton in Abuja where we were having dinner. I connected with him and he was very excited about my leadership journey and successes, expressing an almost unbelievable interest. I was happy to meet him but knew nothing about him beyond that he had been an official in the Lagos State Government.

We exchanged contacts and departed. It is my usual habit to send a text message in the evening of when I meet a new contact, but I failed to send one that day. The following day too. Then the third day he was announced as the running mate of the All

Progressives Congress (APC) presidential candidate. And before I could blink, he was Nigeria's vice president.

Of course I could not begin to reach out at that point because it may have been misconstrued as an artificial attempt to draw close for favors. But imagine that I had reached out the same day we met, that would have cemented the contact and perhaps earned me a sequel meeting before or just after his candidacy announcement. Who knows what may have resulted thereafter? Sure, since then I have met VP Osinbajo a few times, but it was under different circumstances—expectedly.

The act of follow-up is critical in networking. Many times, when you don't follow up, you lose the opportunity. Sometimes, through keeping in touch with someone, you learn about their latest accomplishment. And if your relationship is one of mutual value sharing, who do you think they will share opportunities with in their new office? You will surely be at the top of their list for opportunities within your areas of strength. Imagine if someone you connected with five years ago is now the CEO of a major corporation in your country—or even in his own country, if you are of different nationalities. If you kept in touch, that is an edge for you. But if you didn't, trying to establish contact at this point would be a creep, and you'd be considered a parasite or pest. I recall that there were people who started calling me when I ran for governor of Imo State, Nigeria, in 2019, people who never called me for years. Keeping in touch is the secret to staying relevant in the networking space.

3. Keep Your Competition Close

Contrary to popular opinion, learn to network with your competition. People avoid their perceived enemies, but sometimes the best strategy you may exercise is to network with such people. Being close to them allows you to monitor what they are about. You can even network and collaborate with your competitor to win against a bigger competition. There are different dimensions to it. Be strategic. Don't only network with people you are close to or like; you can learn something from your enemy.

4. Know and Celebrate Their Special Days

When you meet people, make an effort to discover special dates in their lives such as birthdays, wedding anniversaries, children's birthdays, and the like. These days are very important to some people, so reaching out to celebrate with them on such days can add layers to your relationship. Many people feel honored and respected when you contact them on their birthday or travel to attend their special event. The people you contact, visit, or show up for will appreciate it, I assure you.

You need to go beyond initial contact to keeping in touch and retaining your network, so set up measures for knowing, tracking, and celebrating people's special days. The internet is your friend for this. You can research their special days online, then set a reminder for each on Google Calendar or other similar apps. And don't procrastinate, don't put off this step for later, start immediately. Identify fifty people in your network right now and research their special days before the end of this week. Then schedule the dates on your calendar and make it a habit to reach out to them on those days.

5. Say Thank You for Everything

To maximize networking, learn to say "Thank you" at every chance. We live in a time when people act entitled. Yet, it actually doesn't hurt to say thank you. The two-word phrase is simple yet very powerful. It can unlock people's hearts toward you in unimaginably positive ways. Learn to wield this power phrase. You have nothing to lose, but a lot to gain.

Examples of how to phrase your thank you include: "Thank you for your time," "Thank you for seeing me," "Thank you for everything," "Thank you for this meeting," "Thank you for taking my call," "Thank you for the document, it was helpful," etc. Many people take this simple gesture of gratitude for granted, so adopting the habit will distinguish you from others. It projects you as an appreciative person; and because people like to feel appreciated for gestures, they will be drawn to do more for you when you appreciate the little—even more so because very few people take the time to express their thanks.

The power of saying thank you is one of the ingredients that keeps relationships thriving. I'll give you an example. About twenty-five years ago, five families accepted and supported me through school. Many years later, once in every three months I send a text message thanking them for the opportunities they gave me at life. And whenever I meet them in person, I am mindful to still say thank you. Many years after the act of kindness, they still appreciate that I thank them, even though they try to dissuade me oftentimes.

Sometimes I even share the experiences I had with these people on national TV. I remember a particular day when I shared the experiences I had with one of them on TV and someone called the man to inform him of it. He was amazed and called me, perhaps wondering what sort of a man I am.

In these days when people forget favors faster than they receive them, many people are getting weary of helping others. So to stand out, be quick and consistent to thank people, even for the seemingly insignificant things. And when you have the opportunity, accompany your appreciation with a gift. These two acts combined will work wonders for you, believe me.

6. The Power of Confidentiality

A core component of networking is keeping secrets, being confidential. Confidentiality means that if someone gives you access to their space and you have an opportunity to be in a relationship with them, keep to yourself any and all information that no one else should know about. It also means that if the relationship ever crashes, whatever happened within the period of that relationship, good or bad, must remain unsaid. This is a powerful secret for networking upward. People like to keep both their neat wardrobe and dirty laundry private, so if you become privy to their affairs based on the relationship you share, they expect you to keep everything to yourself.

This is why people tend to be cautious before committing or opening up. You need to be a person others can trust. And when they eventually trust you, don't betray them; they will shut you out faster than you think, which may also carry serious repercussions.

Interestingly, what bigmouthed people don't realize is that when you reveal something you shouldn't have, you are actually embarrassing yourself more than the other person. You are also showcasing your untrustworthiness, thereby shutting the door to future networking opportunities for yourself. Nobody wants to associate with a "licky mouth," and they will make it clear to you. Do not betray a confidence. Keep privileged information confidential. Remember, trust is a social asset.

Positioning Your Brand Post-Networking

Now, after you have applied the playbook rules of networking, how do you position your brand post-networking? How do you position yourself to leverage and maximize the potential opportunities that networking breeds? The following are four guiding principles to adopt.

1. Be Excellent

One clearly important principle is that your brand must be excellent. You must deliver on the persona you presented your brand to be. You must uphold and sustain the value perception you created. You must be excellent in your words, actions, and service delivery. You must be authentic.

This is why you must be sincere while networking. Don't project or present who you are not. That is self-sabotage. It is shooting yourself in the foot. If you present a front that you cannot maintain, your subterfuge will inevitably be discovered, sooner or later. Then you will be tagged a fraud and people will remove you from their network.

Now you may be wondering, what if, in your sincerity, your social cadre is not up to the standard of those you are networking with? Again, this is why you must be authentic. You should be authentic regardless. It may interest you to know that the accomplished people you are trying to connect with can oftentimes perceive that you are still on the rising pad of life. If you meet an accomplished person, they often already know that you are on your growth path, still hustling—if you are. As such, what you need is to present yourself well, authentically, and they will want to connect with you. After all, inasmuch as they know you need a push, they too have needs and may need your help based on the value you have. People love good carriage and value. Therefore, know your worth, the value you have to offer as discussed earlier, then sell it correctly when you network with people who are in a better placement than you.

2. Your Product or Service Must Provide Value

What's the use of a product or service that holds no real value to the people it is being promoted to? That is a waste of valuable time and effort. Let the value you present be something your contacts need, then be consistent with providing it once they buy into it. This is why networking should be deliberately value-driven. Your networking efforts should always be guided by the value you have to offer. So be careful to find the people who need it most and connect with them. That way, you are sure to maximize the gains of networking.

3. Your Product or Service Must Be Readily Available

Imagine what a turn-off it would be for a contact who buys into your value offering but cannot get it whenever they need it because you are unable to produce or deliver what you claim to offer. Sooner or later they will tag you as unserious and shift their focus elsewhere. So, promise and always deliver. People want what they want whenever they want it. Never forget that.

4. Your Product or Service Must Be Affordable to Your Target Market

Yes, affordability is important. But of course, affordability is relative. What is affordable to one is expensive to another. And there is also the principle of perceived value, which implies that a customer's buying decision is informed by how they perceive the worth of a product or service in relation to its cost. Therefore, you must be careful to project the value perception you want your target audience to have of your product or service as well as make sure it is affordable to them based on their purchasing power.

Summary Thoughts

1. It is to your detriment if you neglect or disregard networking. Networking is planting a seed today that could yield unimaginably great fruits in the future.

2. Networking is like making deposits in a futuristic, invisible bank account that you can make big withdrawals from on demand.

3. How many people have you connected with in the past but have not spoken to in the last three to five years?

4. The act of follow-up is critical in networking. Many times when you don't follow up, you lose the opportunity.

5. To maximize networking, learn to say "Thank you" at every chance.

6. People like to keep both their neat wardrobe and dirty laundry private, so if you become privy to their affairs based on the relationship you share, they expect you to keep what you know to yourself.

7. Let the value you present be something your contacts need, then be consistent with providing it once they buy into it.

8. Your networking efforts should always be guided by the value you have to offer; be careful to find the people who need it most and connect with them.

ACTIONABLE TAKEAWAYS JOURNAL

CHAPTER 7

HANDLING REJECTION
IN NETWORKING

When Jia Jiang was six years old, one day his first grade teacher came up with a brilliant idea to make her pupils experience the exciting feeling of receiving gifts alongside learning the virtue of complimenting people. She bought enough gifts to go round, stacked them on a table to the side of the classroom, then called all the students to the front of the class. The instruction was to walk to the table and collect your gift after someone complimented you. Excitedly, the 40 kids in the class started complimenting each other and going for their gifts before returning to their seats. One by one, the front of the class started to depopulate until there remained three six-year-olds who didn't get any compliments.

Even worse, nobody seemed to be willing to give them any compliments. Jia was one of them. Freaked out, the teacher asked them to go get their gifts and return to their seats. According to

Jia, she appeared disappointed at what happened to the three kids, which she didn't foresee. She could feel their pain of rejection. And unfortunately, that incident sowed a lifelong seed of fear of rejection in Jia—until he aggressively learned to conquer it many years later.

At age 16, Jia moved to the United States from his home country of China. He had big dreams of becoming an entrepreneur in the future. However, when that future came, he realized that he was always sabotaging or backing down from opportunities at the slightest opposition. The story was no different when he started his own company than when he was an employee.

Exasperated at the limitation that the fear of rejection adopted from his six-year-old self was placing on his life, Jia came up with a plan to aggressively combat the fear. In his research for how to overcome the menace, he stumbled upon Jason Comely's website that presented a rejection therapy game to build confidence and overcome the fear of rejection. Comely recommended deliberately seeking rejection for 30 straight days.[18] Jia decided to go 100 days. He wanted to beat that devil for good, and he came up with daring tasks to achieve. He also decided to film and vlog his journey.

The task for day 1 was to borrow $100 from a stranger. He got to the office that day and during his break time, he went downstairs, saw a chubby security man sitting at his post and decided to approach him.

"Hey, sir, can I borrow a hundred dollars from you?" he asked.

The big guy looked up and said, "No...why?"

Frightened, Jia apologized, turned around and ran away, back to his office.

The idea of the experiment was to review each day's rejection at the end of the day, learn the lessons and desensitize from the pain. So that evening when he assessed what happened, he realized that his biggest problem was that he had allowed the fear of rejection to cripple him all his life, so much that running had become his default response. Another striking thing was the fact that the guy gave him an opportunity to explain himself, he opened room for a conversation, but Jia was too wimpy to engage and ran away instead. That night he decided he would not run again, no matter what happened. He decided he would stay and engage. And that is what he did subsequently.

Day 2 task was to ask for a burger refill. He went to a burger store, finished lunch, went to the cashier and asked, "Hi, can I get a burger refill?"

Puzzled, the cashier asked, "What's a burger refill?"

"Well, just like a drink refill, but with a burger," Jia answered.

"Sorry, we don't do burger refill, man."

Jia didn't quit this time. He continued, "Well, I love your burger, I love your joint; and if you guys do burger refill, I will love you guys more."

Contemplative, the cashier responded, "Okay, I'll tell my manager about it. Maybe we'll do it, but sorry, we can't do this today."

Now, notice that the second day was many times an improvement on the first day. This time he stayed engaged; he didn't turn and run or walk away. That was a significant move. He stayed with the conversation until it reached its logical close. Then he walked away feeling satisfied that he gave it his best shot.

The third day, he planned to ask for a doughnut the shape and colors of the Olympic logo. He went to Krispy Kreme (a chain of doughnut stores most popular in the Southeastern parts of the United States) and asked for a doughnut the shape and colors of the Olympic symbol. This meant interlinking five doughnuts together. Of course, the attendant had never seen, thought of, or made anything like that before, but to his surprise she took him seriously. She asked questions to clarify what he wanted, thought hard for how to achieve it, then went to make it.

Fifteen minutes later, Jia Jiang had a doughnut the shape and colors of the Olympic symbol. This was where his life started to change, he confessed later on a video that gained more than five million views on YouTube. Suddenly Jia was a popular guy. Nevertheless, he made sure to keep his focus. He was in this for the learning and to permanently defeat the fear of rejection, so he made sure fame didn't distract him.

At that point, Jia turned his 100 days of rejection experiment into a research project for how to deal with rejection and turn it into opportunity every time. Expectedly, it turned out to be a life-transforming learning journey for him as he learned so much about rejection: its causes, gains, how to turn a no into a yes, etc.

Ultimately, using his discoveries, Jia now teaches people how to embrace rejection and turn it into opportunities for advancing their lives and fulfilling their dreams. He uses his blog, speaking engagements, a best-selling published book, *Rejection Proof*, and even custom software to teach people how to overcome the fear of rejection.[19]

Jia advises:

The people who really change the world, who change the way we live and the way we think, are people who were met with initial and often violent rejection. People like Martin Luther King Jr., Mahatma Gandhi, Nelson Mandela, or even Jesus Christ. These people did not let rejection define them. They let their own reaction after rejection define them. They embraced rejection...When you get rejected in life, when you are facing the next obstacle or the next failure, consider the possibilities. Don't run. If you just embrace them, they might become your gift.[20]

Fear Is a Thief

Nothing steals away opportunities like fear—fear of failing, of rejection, of not measuring up or being good enough, of disappointment, etc. Fear is a thief. It corrupts your chances of making progress in life. It cripples your heart from believing and taking action—and action is a precondition for progress. Opportunities present themselves, but you must act on them to profit from them. Fear is the greatest undoing of many people with regard to leveraging the power of networking for advancing their lives.

As we established before, you must be proactive at networking. Many networking opportunities come unannounced. Oftentimes you meet people at unexpected places such as the airport, a lounge, during an office visit, a restaurant, parking lot, plane, a casual hangout, etc. Hence, you must be geared up to seize such opportunities quickly to maximize their potential gains. But how can you if you let the fear of rejection handicap you?

Yes, there are times when a person you're considering to connect with at an event seems to have an unfriendly demeanor. Or perhaps the person is highly placed in society. As a result, your heart cringes in fear, assuming the person will not as much as answer your "Hello" if you make the move. But—that is only some hypothesis in your head, an assumption. And many times if you make the move, you find that your assumption was totally wrong. Many times it is that thief called fear trying to steal away yet another opportunity from you—like the countless other ones it has in the past. But—unless you trample on your fear and make the move, you will never know what would actually happen, whether you would have made the connection or not. The only way to know for sure is to act in spite of your fear. As the old axiom goes, feel the fear but do it anyhow!

Interestingly, as discussed earlier, most people you try to network with often understand the importance and power of networking. In fact, chances are high that networking played a key role in their journey to becoming who they are today. And they aren't stopping anytime soon. Like you, they are still evolving into their best selves, so they are open to meeting new people who could prove valuable to them. Remember the rule is to come with value to provide. If you do, there is a very good chance that you will not be rejected. And wear confidence in your approach, not timidity.

In essence, networking is a bargain for mutual benefits. So, there is really no reason to fear. You want something, the other person wants something, so what you both need is to converse and determine if the value each person has is a need to the other. If yes, there is business to be done—immediately or later.

Of course, the opportunities of networking and their timing are as diverse as there are people who engage in it. Therefore, a person who doesn't exactly seem to have value you need in the immediate could have something huge for you tomorrow, maybe a simple referral that could do you a lot of good. Again, conquer your fears!

How to Respond to Rejection in Networking

One of the reasons people don't take the first step in networking is the fear of rejection. Sometimes, it is temperament-induced. This especially applies to introverts, yet it is not an excuse. Whatever your temperament, you must learn how to handle rejection during an attempt at networking. You could meet someone who might insult you, tell you off, speak to you rudely or condescendingly, or speak negatively to you with their body language. What do you do in such situations? Are these the norm? Absolutely not. Still, they are possibilities, unfortunately, so we must learn how to deal with rejection. I offer the following four ways to deal with rejection:

1. Never take it personally, even if it seems personal.

Discomforting as it is, the smart thing to do if you get rejected is to not take it personally. That is, don't assume in your mind that it is because of you or something you did wrong that you were rejected. Don't take it as a blight on your person, as if you are not good enough. Instead, it could actually be a reason tied to the other person. Maybe they are in a bad mood. Maybe they have an emergency or deliverable that is preoccupying their mind. Maybe they have a challenge they are dealing with in that moment. In other words, make an excuse for the person in your mind. Don't take the turn-down personally.

In Jia Jiang's experiments, one day he knocked on a stranger's door and asked to plant a flower in his backyard. Blankly, the guy said no. But having learned some valuable lessons from his journey till that point, Jia didn't just walk away, he politely asked why. Then the guy explained that his dog had a habit of digging up whatever he planted in his backyard, and he didn't want to waste the plant. Even more, contrary to Jia's expectation, the man referred him to a lady across the street who liked flowers. He went over to her house, knocked, and she happily let him plant the flower in her backyard.

What if Jia walked away immediately after the first stranger said no? He would have left making up reasons in his mind for why he got rejected, and most likely he would have blamed himself for it. But notice that the real reason had *nothing* to do with him; it was all on the guy. So again, when someone rejects you, don't take it personally. You will be needlessly harming yourself emotionally.

I remember one time I was attending an economic summit and I approached a young woman to network with. She was attractive and professional in her carriage, but she ignored me. Without losing a moment, I excused her in my mind as probably not in the right mood. I went on to network with other people in the room, and one of them turned out to be her boss. When she approached me later, the boss called me by my first name as we were parting. Later the woman apologized and gave reasons why she acted unwelcoming to me. I told her it was no problem, I wasn't offended. I had given an excuse for her in my mind.

2. Analyze why the rejection happened and learn from your mistakes.

Sometimes networkers are rejected because of how they present themselves. Sometimes they may be inappropriately forward, which turns the person off. Some networkers do not read their target's mood. A trick to use sometimes is to "flash a smile," if there is a response, that is a sign that the person is open for an approach.

Furthermore, it should be obvious to others that you care about your appearance. Being poorly dressed and/or having an offensive odor is an image breaker, and no one wants to connect with that. The subliminal message people see is that you have little or no value to offer. If it seems you don't care about how you look and smell, you won't be trusted to produce excellent value. Don't sabotage yourself when you want to build a great network for results. Do it right. Start with the basics of looking, smelling, and speaking well.

3. Be persistent and keep coming back.

Sometimes people's knowledge of you might be limited, so be persistent. Be strategic about it. Don't pose as a pest; you will shut the door to yourself permanently. If there are people you have purposed to meet because of the value they potentially hold for your vision, if they reject you the first time, return to your drawing table and re-strategize about how to connect with them again. Stay at it. And remember to approach from an angle of value that they need. Sooner or later, you will get on their radar and build a good bond.

4. Move to other people or places where you can be accepted.

As I shared in the example, the young woman turned me down and I moved on to others who accepted me. It is important that networking becomes part of our daily lives. Never succumb to rejection; it is simply a temporary setback. Rejection is not a curse, so don't make it one for you.

How to Overcome Fear: The Power of Hope

In 1957, Curt Richter, a Harvard graduate and Johns Hopkins University professor of biology, conducted an experiment to determine resilience, using domestic and wild rats. The experiments proved to be quite interesting and insightful, revealing the power of hope to fuel resilience. It involved placing the rats in buckets filled with water and testing how long they could survive before drowning.

Richter experimented with domesticated rats as well as wild rats and they produced different results. A total of twelve domestic rats were used for the first experiments. One by one, each were placed into the water-filled bucket and the different results recorded. The first three rats swam around on the surface before giving up and going under. They lasted underwater for about two minutes before giving up and drowning. The other nine rats, on the other hand, mostly stuck to the surface of the water and this helped them to last for hours before drowning from exhaustion.

The second round of the experiment involved 34 wild rats. These rats were placed in water-filled buckets like the domesticated rats, but despite their ferocity and fitness, not one of them lasted past a few minutes. To Richter, the domestic rats were able to survive for a longer period because of the presence of hope and anticipated aid from the humans they were familiar with, while the wild rats that were used to a system of kill-or-be-killed did not bother to hold out because there was no hope in view for them.

To further prove this hypothesis, Richter conducted a fresh set of experiments. This time he picked a new set of rats not segregated by habitat and subjected them to another bucket of water. However, just as they were about to drown, he pulled them out, cleaned them up and allowed them time to rest and recover. Then he put them back into the water.

Strangely, the second time they went into the water, they lasted much longer, threading the water for 60 hours—two days and a half—before succumbing to exhaustion. Curt determined from this experiment that the third set of rats survived much longer because of the hope inspired in them by the temporary time out of the water the first time.[21] That is, knowing that there was a possibility of another escape as before, hopelessness was dispelled and they were resilient. In other words, because the rats felt they had a fighting chance, the hope and possibility of being saved kept them fighting for 60 hours nonstop. In the words of Curt Richter, "the rats quickly learn that the situation is not actually hopeless" and that, "after elimination of hopelessness the rats do not die."[22]

The lesson for networking in this experiment is to always focus on the reward, not the temporary setback or rejection that may occur. Think back to the wins you may have had in the past from strategic networking, whether you directly orchestrated it or not. Reflect on how much impact someone you connected with in the past has had on your life so far. Now, how much more progress will you make if you have more of such people in your life? Is that end result worth the effort to grow your network? If yes, let that hope overpower any fears you may have. In the end, the result justifies the process. Never stop networking.

Summary Thoughts

1. Fear is a thief. It corrupts your chances of making progress in life.

2. Action is a precondition for progress.

3. Opportunities present themselves, but you must act on them to profit from them.

4. Networking is a bargain for mutual benefits.

5. The smart thing to do if you get rejected is to not take it personally.

6. It should be obvious that you care about how you look. Being poorly dressed and/or having an offensive odor is an image breaker, and no one will want to connect with you.

7. Never succumb to rejection; it is simply a temporary setback.

ACTIONABLE TAKEAWAYS JOURNAL

CONCLUSION

Congratulations on reaching the final chapter of *Networking for Results*. This isn't merely the end of a book; it's the beginning of a transformative journey in your professional and personal life. By engaging with these pages, you've initiated a powerful process: the honing of your networking skills, a craft accessible to anyone willing to invest effort, time, and heart.

I started my journey from humble beginnings, with little more than determination and a belief in the power of human connection. By consciously building and leveraging a network, I transitioned from those beginnings to a life enriched both professionally and personally. I can say, unequivocally, that a well-cultivated network can be a life-altering asset.

If there's one thing to remember, it's this: networking is not a one-time event but a lifelong process. In this ever-evolving landscape, the only constant is your continuous engagement with people around you. Therefore, make a commitment to sustain your efforts, to practise deliberately, and to refine your techniques relentlessly.

I strongly recommend undertaking a candid self-assessment to solidify your commitment and sharpen your focus. Evaluate your networking strengths and acknowledge your weaknesses. Develop an action plan to transform those weak spots into future strengths. Remember, the path to mastery is a marathon, not a sprint.

To ensure this book doesn't just sit on your shelf, at the end of this page you will find a practical checklist of actionable items from what you've learned. Let this be your roadmap, your first step in a lifetime of effective networking.

Should you find that you need tailored guidance or mentorship, I offer one-on-one coaching sessions designed to accelerate your networking skills and enrich your circle of influence. Your growth journey needn't be a solitary one; we can walk parts of it together.

As you implement these strategies and start seeing success, I invite you to get in touch with me and share your story. Your journey could serve as invaluable inspiration for others.

Thank you for entrusting me with your time and attention. It's a privilege to contribute to your journey towards networking mastery. As you turn this page, you're not closing a book but opening a new chapter in your life. I wish you unparalleled success in all your networking endeavours.

Dr. Linus Okorie MFR

PRACTICAL CHECKLIST FOR EFFECTIVE NETWORKING

✔ Identify Goals: Write down the primary objectives you hope to achieve through networking (e.g., job opportunities, collaborations, etc.).

✔ Research: Prioritise your top 10 networking targets (people or organisations). Learn about their work, needs, and how you can offer value.

✔ Elevator Pitch: Craft a 30-second introduction that encapsulates who you are, what you do, and what value you can bring to a professional relationship.

✔ Reach Out: Contact at least three people from your network every week to either establish or strengthen your connection.

✔ Follow-Up: After any networking event or meaningful conversation, send a personalised follow-up message within 48 hours.

✔ Value Offer: Identify and list ways you can offer value to your connections. Aim to offer something valuable at least once a month.

✔ Organise Contacts: Use a system (app, spreadsheet, etc.) to track your networking activities, including when you last contacted each person and any upcoming opportunities to reconnect.

✔ Ask for Introductions: Don't be shy about asking existing contacts for introductions to others who can help you achieve your networking goals.

✔ Regular Check-In: At the end of each month, review your networking goals, the connections you've made, and the value you've offered or received. Adjust your actions accordingly for the next month.

ENDNOTES

1. https://wikifarmer.com/orange-tree-harvest-and-yields/#:~:-
   text=The%20average%20healthy%20and%20mature,to%20
   600%20oranges%20per%20tree; accessed January 16, 2023.

2. Dele Momodu: https://en.wikipedia.org/wiki/Dele_Momodu;
   accessed September 14, 2023.

3. Ngozi Okonji Iweala: https://en.wikipedia.org/wiki/Ngozi_
   Okonjo-Iweala; accessed September 14, 2023.

4. Tony Onyemachi Elumelu: https://en.wikipedia.org/wiki/
   Tony_Elumelu ; accessed September 14, 2023.

5. Patrick Utomi: https://en.wikipedia.org/wiki/Patrick_Utomi;
   accessed September 14, 2023.

6. Nduka Obaigbena: https://en.wikipedia.org/wiki/Nduka_
   Obaigbena; accessed September 14, 2023.

7. Ibrahim Badamasi Babangida: https://en.wikipedia.org/wiki/ Ibrahim_Babangida; accessed September 14, 2023.

8. Late Raymond Dokpesi: https://en.wikipedia.org/wiki/Raymond_Dokpesi#:~:text=He%20d id%20his%20undergraduate%20studies,sponsored%20by%20Alhaji%20Bamanga%20 Tukur; accessed September 14, 2023.

9. John Donne (157201631), "No Man Is an Island"; https://allpoetry.com/No-man-is-an-island; accessed January 16, 2023.

10. Luke 6:38, The Passion Translation.

11. Adebola Williams; https://en.wikipedia.org/wiki/Adebola_Williams; accessed January 16, 2023.

12. Mfonobong Nsehe, "Meet the 30-Year-Old Nigerian Entrepreneur Who Helped 3 African Presidents Get Elected," *Forbes*, February 17, 2017; https://www.forbes.com/sites/ mfonobongnsehe/2017/02/17/meet-the-30-year-old-nigerian-entrepreneur-who-helped-3-african-presidents-get-elected/?sh=5ea5b5b27df8; accessed January 16, 2023.

13. Alamu Tosin, "Adebola Williams Biography, Net Worth, Father, Wife, Family, Instagram, Facts," *NGNews247*, August 9, 2021; https://www.ngnews247.com/adebola-williams-biography-net-worth-father-wife-family-instagram-facts/; accessed January 16, 2023.

14. Shana Lebowitz, et.al., "Inside the over 30-year friendship of Bill Gates and Warren Buffett, who didn't even want

to meet at first but now have each other on speed dial," *BusinessInsider*, December 20, 2022; https://www.businessinsider.com/bill-gates-warren-buffett-friendship-2018-3; accessed January 17, 2023.

15. Omar Abdel-Baqui, "Giving Pledge Grows as More of World's Wealthy Sign On to Give Away Money," *The Wall Street Journal*, December 14, 2021; https://www.wsj.com/articles/giving-pledge-grows-as-more-of-worlds-wealthy-sign-on-to-give-away-money-11639505058; accessed January 17, 2023.

16. "Warren Buffet Profile," *Forbes*, January 17, 2023; https://www.forbes.com/profile/warren-buffett/?sh=6da939a84639; accessed January 17, 2023.

17. Tom Huddleston Jr., "What you need to know about Greg Abel—Warren Buffett's successor at Berkshire Hathaway"; *CNBC.com*, May 3, 2021; https://www.cnbc.com/2021/05/03/who-is-greg-abel-warren-buffetts-successor-at-berkshire-hathaway.html; accessed January 17, 2023.

18. Rejection Therapy game; https://www.rejectiontherapy.com/game/; accessed January 17, 2023.

19. Jia Jiang's website: https://www.rejectiontherapy.com/; accessed January 17, 2023.

20. *TED Talk*, Jia Jiang, May 2015; https://www.youtube.com/watch?v=-vZXgApsPCQ; accessed January 17, 2023.

21. Sheikh Sabbir, "Drowning Rats Psychology Experiment: Resilience and the Power of Hope," *Medium.com*; https:// sabbirsk1560.medium.com/drowning-rats-psychology-experiment-resilience-and-the-power-of-hope-47725942d902; accessed January 17, 2023.

22. *World of Work*, "A Psychology Experiment: Drowning Rats," July 2019; https://worldofwork.io/2019/07/drowning-rats-psychology-experiments/; accessed January 17, 2023.

ABOUT THE AUTHOR

Linus Okorie is a member of faculty at the GOTNI Leadership Centre. He is a renowned leadership development coach and human capital development consultant. For more than twenty years, he has been known as a relentless icon in the quest for good leadership in public and corporate governance in Nigeria. His vast experience in leadership coaching, mentoring, and advocacy worldwide has distinguished him as a trusted name in leadership excellence.

Linus Okorie is the founder and president or the Guardians of the Nation International (GOTNI), a leadership development nonprofit organization, which has developed fifteen leadership brands to train and nurture youths, elected officials, and the general public on effective leadership skills and values. Consistently, Linus Okorie has carved a niche as an authority in leadership development with a career development path defined by the principles of selfless service, dignity, and integrity.

Since inception, Linus Okorie has piloted GOTNI to become Nigeria's foremost leadership capital development organization including the establishment of GOTNI Leadership Centre (GLC) in Jabi, Abuja. He is currently working toward building the much anticipated Global Leadership Centre at the Oguta Lake, Imo State where excellent leaders will be groomed for the growth and development of Nigeria and the African continent. He is pioneering the emergence of a new breed of well-equipped and competent leaders to filtrate the public and private sector hierarchies in Nigeria and the rest of Africa.

As an influential speaker, Linus Okorie has graced many live conferences, radio and television platforms across Africa, Middle East, Europe, and the USA as guest speaker, trainer, and advisor. He is the author of *Footprints: Leading Beyond Today*, Foreword written by Dr. Myles Munroe.

Linus Okorie earned a Master's degree in Organizational Leadership from Regent University, Virginia Beach, USA. He is an alumnus of the International Visitors Program (IVLP) sponsored by the US government under the Department of State. He is also an alumnus of the Executive Leadership Education program of Harvard University's Kennedy School of Government, Boston, USA with a certification in The Act and Practice of Leadership Development.

Linus hails from UmuEzike-egbu, Egbuoma in Oguta Local Government Area of Imo State. He is married to Nkiru with whom he has two daughters and a son.

For more enriching content and insights, all books authored by Linus Okorie MFR are available for purchase on Amazon. Simply scan the QR code below to directly access the complete list. Your journey to leadership excellence is just a scan away!

OTHER BOOKS AUTHORED BY LINUS OKORIE MFR

Footprints: Leading Beyond Today
Foreword by Dr. Myles Munroe

Footprints: Leading Beyond Today is a holistic leadership guide to equip you with the inspiration, information, skills, and qualities you need to live a life of outstanding leadership—every day in any circumstance. Your impact, contributions, and legacy will live beyond today.

Footprints is packed with practical insights that break down the broad subject of leadership into comprehensible components and simplistic formats that inspire, motivate, and transform.

Your leadership talents will be awakened, your potential stirred, and your skills honed so you can be the best leader you can be. The leadership principles and qualities taught cut across every walk of life because everyone is meant to lead right within their spheres of influence.

The Economics of Leadership
Foreword by Prof. Greg Ibe

With a focus on transformative thought, esteemed leadership expert Dr. Linus Okorie guides readers through essential guidance for navigating unpredictable landscapes.

Discover how effective leadership drives economic growth, fosters innovation, and positions organizations and nations for success. Through real-world examples and practical guidance, Dr. Okorie empowers leaders to:

- Make tough decisions that lead to long-term success.
- Forge strategic partnerships to maximize resources.
- Foster a culture of innovation and adaptability.
- Position organizations for growth and prosperity.

This book serves as a valuable resource for leaders at all levels who are seeking to create lasting legacies and overcome challenges in today's ever-changing world.

GET IN TOUCH WITH
DR. LINUS OKORIE MFR

linusokorie.net

info@linusokorie.net

/drlinusokorie

/LinusOkori1

@linusokorie1

/linus-okorie-19b33544

+234 903 810 5300

Publishing Services by
EVANGELISTA MEDIA & CONSULTING

publisher@evangelistamedia.com
www.evangelistamedia.com

 /evangelistamediaconsulting

 evangelista_media_consulting

www.ingramcontent.com/pod-product-compliance
Lightning Source LLC
Chambersburg PA
CBHW070017300526
45794CB00001B/348